# IMITATING THE SAINTS:
## CHRISTIAN PHILOSOPHY AND SUPERHERO MYTHOLOGY

## Adam Barkman

**Imitating the Saints:**
Christian Philosophy and Superhero Mythology

Copyright © 2013 Adam Barkman

Winged Lion Press
Hamden, CT

All rights reserved. Except in the case of quotations embodied in critical articles or reviews, no part of this book may be reproduced or transmitted in any form or by any means, electronic or mechanical, including photocopying, recording, or by any information storage or retrieval system, without written permission of the publisher.
For information, contact Winged Lion Press www.WingedLionPress.com

Winged Lion Press titles may be purchased for business or promotional use or special sales.

Cover Design: Ashley Barkman

10-9-8-7-6-5-4-3-2-1

WINGED LION PRESS

ISBN-13  978-1-935688-05-1

# ACKNOWLEDGEMENTS

I would like to thank Redeemer University College for providing me with grants not only to research this project but also to edit and index it, and I would like to thank Ashley Barkman for helping me prepare the MS.

I must acknowledge that the images contained in this book belong to DC and Marvel and I'm grateful to be able to use them.

Finally, most of the chapters in this book were published elsewhere in one form or another. This material includes:

"The Political Legacy of Superheroes." *Comment* (Spring 2012): 101-107.

"*Gladiator*, Gender and Marriage in Heaven: A Christian Exploration." In *The Culture and Philosophy of Ridley Scott*. Edited by Adam Barkman, Ashley Barkman and Nancy Kang. Lanham, MD: Lexington Books, 2013. A version was also published in *Above All Things: Essays on Christian Ethics and Popular Culture*. Hamden, CT: Winged Lion, 2011.

"Superman: From Anti-Christ to Christ-Type." *In Superman and Philosophy*. Edited by Mark White. Hoboken, NJ: Wiley, 2013. A version was also published in *Above All Things: Essays on Christian Ethics and Popular Culture*. Hamden, CT: Winged Lion, 2011.

"The Ring of Gyges, the Ring of the Green Lantern and the Temptation of Power." In *Green Lantern and Philosophy*. Edited by Mark White and Jane Dryden. Hoboken, NJ: Wiley, 2011. A version was also published in *Through Common Things: Philosophical Reflections on Global Popular Culture*. Hamden, CT: Winged Lion, 2010.

"'No Other Gods Before Me': God, Ontology and Ethics in the Avengers' Universe." In *Avengers and Philosophy*. Edited by Mark White. Hoboken, NJ: Wiley, 2012. A version was also published in *Above All Things: Essays on Christian Ethics and Popular Culture*. Hamden, CT: Winged Lion, 2011.

"'The Power to Go Beyond God's Boundaries'? Hulk, Human Nature and Some Ethical Concerns Thereof." In *The Philosophy of Ang Lee*. Edited by Robert Arp, Adam Barkman and James McRae. Lexington, KT: University Press of Kentucky, 2013. A version was also published in *Above All Things: Essays on Christian Ethics and Popular Culture*. Hamden, CT: Winged Lion, 2011.

"'With Great Power Comes Great Responsibility': Spider-Man, Christian Ethics and the Problem of Evil." In *Spider-Man and Philosophy*. Edited by Jonathan Sanford. Hoboken, NJ: Wiley, 2012. A version was also published in *Through Common Things: Philosophical Reflections on Global Popular Culture*. Hamden, CT: Winged Lion, 2010.

*To Tristan*

*Since you were very young, I have seen you desire, and "try really hard," to become a man of justice and sacrificial love. Of course, no one, save for Christ, does this perfectly, but you have not disappointed me in your realization that the most important aspect of the moral life, and life in general, is to speak justice to God—to say you're sorry—and then attempt to live this out. Insofar as you have endeavored to develop in these ways, there is, as Captain says to Hulk, "a word for someone like you—hero." And it is your father's prayer you ever remain and continue to grow as one.*

 *God bless you, my precious son,*
 *Dad*

# TABLE OF CONTENTS

| | | |
|---|---|---|
| INTRODUCTION | Christian Philosophy and Superhero Mythology | 1 |
| CHAPTER 1 | The Political Legacy of Superheroes | 25 |
| CHAPTER 2 | Gender, Disability and Superheroes | 35 |
| CHAPTER 3 | Superman: From Anti-Christ to Christ-Type | 61 |
| CHAPTER 4 | Green Lantern: Willpower, Not Will-To-Power | 77 |
| CHAPTER 5 | The Avengers: Good Gods | 89 |
| CHAPTER 6 | The Hulk: Identity and "God's Boundaries" | 103 |
| CHAPTER 7 | Spider-Man: Power and Responsibility | 113 |
| INDEX | | 125 |

# INTRODUCTION

## CHRISTIAN PHILOSOPHY AND SUPERHERO MYTHOLOGY

The title of this book, *Imitating the Saints: Christian Philosophy and Superhero Mythology*, neither was accidentally chosen nor, sadly, is clear in meaning. Nevertheless, it is my hope that when both phrases in the subtitle—"Christian philosophy" and "superhero mythology"—are unpacked, the title, and with it, the general direction of this book, will come into greater focus.

### A CHRISTIAN PHILOSOPHY OF MYTHOLOGY

As soon as a human person is able to demonstrate his rationality, he finds himself believing certain key things about the world such that we can say that this person has a worldview. Accordingly, the Hindu child will believe in a Hindu worldview, for example, and the Christian in a Christian one, and both, at least at an early age, are rationally justified in their respective beliefs. Indeed, insofar as these very situated people begin to think hard and pursue truth in some measure, these people can be seen to be doing philosophy.

Nevertheless, while there are many perspectives on things, there is only one truth of the matter, truth being the agreement or correspondence between propositions and reality. The proposition "Brahma is the creator deity" might be thought to be true from within a Hindu worldview and yet thought to be false from within the Christian one, and while both might be wrong, both, by the rules of contrariety, can't be true at the same time when the terms are understood in the same way. If, however, a proposition connected to Brahma, such as "The world was made by a deity," is true, then we can see that Hinduism agrees with Christianity, which also asserts this proposition, and so truth (if this proposition is indeed true) can be found in both worldviews. Yet even so, it's highly unlikely that any two worldviews would assert the same amount of true propositions on all fundamental beliefs, implying, therefore, that some worldviews will be truer than others. My claim, as a Christian philosopher, is that though far from complete and perfect, the (for lack of a better word) orthodox or mere Christian worldview contains the most true propositions of any worldview.

Thus when I use the phrase "Christian philosophy," I refer not only to the activity that seeks out and desires to consider all things that can be known—all evidence, including the evidence unique to Christianity—but also the activity that finds the general Christian presentation of things the most rationally compelling. Philosophers are truth-seekers, and Christian philosophers are those that think that in addition to everything else that is true, the Bible is also an important—a very important—fount of truth. Moreover, because truth is one, all true beliefs are connected in some way,[1] and so the Christian philosopher is very concerned with seeing how evidence from the Bible (special revelation) and evidence from other sources (general revelation) connect and complement each other.

The Christian philosopher, then, far from being afraid of truth, is passionate about it and isn't put off by the disdains of those who, variously, scorn Confucius, Colossians or comic books. For the Christian philosopher, the activities of children and adults alike are worthy of thought and consideration. No stone should remain unturned when truth is the goal, and this includes the stone of mythology.

Now in general, philosophy is the activity of thinking hard about something, and when this activity is done in respect to art and beauty, we call it aesthetics. Aesthetics itself can be sub-divided into many species, one of which is the philosophy of mythology.[2] This is the branch of philosophy that critically examines or theorizes about mythology, and this activity has a long tradition full of colorful figures and intriguing ideas, some of which argue that myths are "lies told by poets" (one view held by Plato),[3] allegories to be dissected for some hidden moral meaning (the Stoics),[4] fun fiction (one

---

[1] As Thomas Aquinas says, "Nothing which implies contradiction falls under the omnipotence of God." Thomas Aquinas *Summa Theologica* Ia, Q. 35, art. 4.

[2] What I call "the philosophy of mythology" has been called many different things. C. S. Lewis, for example, speaks of it as "the science of the nature of myths" or "mythologics." C. S. Lewis, *The Collected Letters of C. S. Lewis: Volume I; Family Letters 1905-1931*, ed. Walter Hooper (London: HarperCollins, 2000), 765.

[3] "And we'll deny the truth of the stories that [Achilles] dragged Hector around Patroclus's tomb and slaughtered prisoners on his funeral pyre. And we won't allow our citizens to believe that Achilles—the child of a goddess and of Peleus (who was himself a model of self-discipline and a grandson of Zeus) and tutored by the sage Cheiron—was so full of turmoil that he suffered from the two conflicting diseases of mean-spirited avarice and disdain for gods and men." Plato *Republic* 391b-c. It should be noted that Plato didn't think that all myths are simply poetic lies; he himself was a masterful mythmaker as we see with the story of the Ring of Gyges, for example. The myths that Plato would approve of, however, are those that communicate truth, and since he thought most of the myths of his day had little to no truth in them, he was largely opposed to mythology.

[4] The Stoics were the ones who popularized the practice of *hyponoia* or the unveiling of hidden meanings in myths; indeed, it was largely with them that this practice became known as *allegoriai* or allegorizing, which is when an individual discards

view held by Macrobius),[5] systems of open-ended metaphors that can mean virtually anything (the School of Chartres),[6] a web of symbols that need to be translated for some hidden sexual meaning (Freud), "the disease of language" (Müller),[7] primitive self-expression which needs to be scientifically clarified (Frazer), and so on. Most philosophers of mythology have claimed that myths are more or less allegories that need to be unpacked for some deeper, more primitive meaning.

Yet in the past century or so, some Christian philosophers of myth, such as G. K. Chesterton, C. S. Lewis and J. R. R. Tolkien, have, without denying that myths can be allegorically read or that myths often have general themes, tried to move discussions of mythology beyond overly simplistic readings. Chesterton, for example, says bluntly, "Myths are not allegories,"[8] and Lewis and Tolkien heartily agree. Moreover, all three of these men approach myth rationally, that is, as philosophers (understood in the broadest possible sense), and all three argue that myth is tremendously important. Needless to say, I borrow heavily from them when I try to explain what I think mythology is.[9]

---

the surface meaning of a text, for instance, "Ulysses's ship," for a deeper, spiritual meaning, such as "the human soul;" as Cicero said of the Stoics, "A great deal of . . . trouble was taken by Zeno [the Stoic], then Cleanthes and lastly by Chrysippus to rationalize these purely fanciful myths and explain the reasons for the names by which the various deities are called." Cicero *On the Nature of the Gods* 3.24.63.

5 "Fables—the very word acknowledges their falsity—serve two purposes: either merely to gratify the ear or to encourage the reader to good works. They delight the ear as do the comedies of Menander and his imitators, or the narratives replete with imaginary doings of lovers in which Petronius Arbiter so freely indulged and with which Apuleius, astonishingly, sometimes amused himself." Macrobius *Commentary on the Dream of Scipio* 1.2.7-8.

6  Winthrop Wetherbee, *Platonism and Poetry in the Twelfth Century: The Literary Influence of the School of Chartres* (Princeton: Princeton University Press, 1972), 13.

7  Max Müller (1823-1900), who is generally regarded as the founder of comparative mythology, and James Frazer (1854-1941) both saw mythology as a primitive stage in the development of human history. Eric Csapo, *Theories of Mythology* (Oxford: Blackwell, 2005), 26, 38. Müller saw poetic language as the natural expression of the simple mind and mythology as the "disease of language," while Frazer, perhaps partially influenced by Auguste Comte, saw human development in terms of three ages: the Age of Magic, the Age of Religion and the Age of Science, wherein the Ages of Magic and Religion (and, of course, mythology) are transcended by scientific or "rational" accounts of the things that mythology, crudely, points to.

8  G. K. Chesterton, *The Everlasting Man* (San Francisco: Ignatius Press, 1993), 104.

9  For those who would like to know more about Lewis's theory of mythology, I recommend chapter four of my book *C. S. Lewis and Philosophy as a Way of Life* (Allentown, PA: Zossima, 2009).

## Imitating the Saints

Chesterton, Lewis and Tolkien all think there is good evidence not only that God exists but also that He is the Creator of all things. God starts the creation and sees to its development according to a very detailed plan. Part of God's plan in creation is to create rational creatures, in particular, man, who has the ultimate capacity not only to reason and choose, but also to create and feel. It is man's ultimate capacity to rationally, self-consciously create that caused Tolkien to speak of man as a "sub-creator"—man the rational creator being made in the image of God the Rational Creator.[10] The ability to create and the ability to feel moved by things created is part of God's design for man.

Moreover, the creative faculty in man and man's emotions toward created things can be either properly functioning or improperly functioning. To create good art is for the imaginative faculty to function well and to create bad art is for it to function badly; to feel moved by good art is for our emotions in respect to this art to be functioning well and to feel unmoved by good art is for our emotions to be malfunctioning in some measure.

While the badness I speak about here is aesthetic badness and emotional badness—neither of which are identical to moral badness, evil, sin or (willed) injustice—moral badness or injustice is often connected with these other types of badness in two ways: the injustice that comes by refusing to use the creative faculty in the first place, and the injustice that comes through misusing the creative faculty.

In respect to the injustice that comes by refusing to use the creative faulty in the first place, if God designed man to create (if man has been given what is sometimes called a "creational" or "cultural mandate"), then for man *not* to create things can be seen, in some cases at least, as injustice since disobedience to God is a form of injustice. Indeed, the Hebrew Bible isn't the only source telling us of God's expectation for man to use his rational and creative faculties well—"to subdue the earth," so to speak: Mesopotamian, Greek, Hindu and even North American mythologies make it clear that deity (variously called Ea, Prometheus, Agni, or Rabbit) expects man to use divine gifts (fire or rational creativity) to flourish and to glorify the deity in this flourishing.

In respect to the injustice that comes through misusing the creative faculty, if the created thing that man makes celebrates (as opposed to reports or, to some higher end, uses) badness of any sort, then there is probably a moral dimension to this as well since in general man has been morally charged with not simply creating, but creating things in keeping with the good—the aesthetic good always, but also, where appropriate, the moral good as well. Of course, "in keeping with the good" is a difficult phrase since nearly everything made by the hand of man is bent to some extent both aesthetically and morally.

---

10  J. R. R. Tolkien, "On Fairy-Stories," in *The Tolkien Reader* (New York: Ballantine, 1975), 22.

## Christian Philosophy and Superhero Mythology

And all art probably has some aesthetic goodness in it and probably exemplifies some moral goodness as well. Thus, what I mean by a good work of art—and so, without getting ahead of myself, a good myth—is one that has a high degree of aesthetic goodness, and, where appropriate, champions, points to or stirs us to reflect upon moral goodness in a particularly effective way. In this respect, at least, I agree with men like Plato and Confucius.

Although all people are created with imaginative and emotive faculties and so all are expected to use these, not all, at least in this life, are probably expected to create and feel to the same extent. Some will be able to sculpt like Michelangelo; some will be able to feel the depths of Bach's "Jesu, Joy of Man's Desiring;" and some will be able recognize the distinction between Starbucks and Tim Horton's; but many will not, and, though not being able to do all these things is in some sense aesthetically wanting, few of these people are likely to be considered morally wanting for this aesthetic lack. Thus, the moral obligation is to try our best, given the particulars of our situation and the priorities before us, to create art and feel toward the created art—including myths—that which is in keeping with the good.

Now some of the things that man the sub-creator makes are myths. In fact, myths are arguably the oldest of man's inventions: they have been with us since the beginning in oral narratives, in music, in paintings and in sculptures. However, the raw materials of myth are ideas that God has eternally known and so are things not created ex nihilo by man, but rather are things that man discovers and then, to some extent, rearranges. Tolkien, in the voice of Aragorn, says that the green earth itself is "a mighty matter of legend,"[11] which is to say that far from being a mere collection of atoms in motion or a dead mechanistic thing, nature is alive—it has *animus*, soul—and therein wonderfully exhibits the dust of divine creation. Shamanistic cultures are not wrong to declare living nature ensouled; their mistake is to see the life of flowers, trees and animals as equal to that of man, who is, in contrast to these, a rational, conditionally immortal soul. And, of course, being a living soul, man himself is also an important ingredient in myth; in fact, Tolkien goes so far as to say that most of the good myths that man tells require the presence of man in order to make the story relatable.[12]

But while enchanted nature and humans are important elements in *most* myths, *all* myths—unlike all epics, legends or tragedies—must have elements of things that are above nature and humanity; myths, in other words, must have a super-natural or super-human element.

---

11  C. S. Lewis reports that this quote is from book three, chapter two of *The Lord of the Rings* (that is, in *The Two Towers*), but I myself couldn't find this precise quote there. See C. S. Lewis, "Tolkien's *The Lord of the Rings*," in *C. S. Lewis: Essay Collection and Other Short Stories*, ed. Lesley Walmsley (London: HarperCollins, 2000), 524.

12  Tolkien, "On Fairy-Stories," 9.

In many biblical stories, some of which we may properly call myths if by that we don't assume them to be necessarily false or unhistorical,[13] the supreme super-human presence is God, who, as per Tolkien's requirement that super-humans do super-human acts, is a great worker of marvels and wonders. God, of course, is a unique figure in that He is both the general author of the great myth called creation, and also a vital character in it. And although rarely explicitly present in non-biblical myths, God still lingers. For instance, in Norse mythology, unchanging Fate—arguably an aspect of God Himself—stands above and beyond even primordial Fire and Ice, and certainly beyond the poorly named "All-Father," Odin. Or again, in ancient Iranian, Indian and Chinese mythology, we read about *Asha*, *Rita* or *Tao*, which is the supreme, unchanging Law that stands above and beyond all the gods—though the gods are often Its servants. If Tolkien is right, and I think he is, in saying that the greatest myths must have a clear sense of good and evil,[14] then what Tolkien could also be seen to be saying is that the greatest myths must have the presence of a supreme good or a supreme moral law, which judges the rightness or wrongness of particular acts. And since this law is best explained by theism,[15] that is, as flowing out of God's character as the Good, it seems reasonable to say that the greatest myths must exhibit, either clearly or darkly, the presence of God.

In addition to, or in place of, the supreme super-human, God, many myths, even biblical ones, have other super-humans. The biblical angels are either good or bad, and more than one Christian theologian, not the least of which is C. S. Lewis, thinks these could properly be called "gods." These lower-case "g" gods—created gods—are, in biblical myth, responsible for many good and bad events in our world. They fight, they worship, they are worshipped, they dwell in the highest realms, they are cast down to the lowest depths, they rebel, they report, and they do many things that the pagans would have recognized to be in keeping with the activities of their gods. The titans in Greek mythology are cast out of the heavens and imprisoned in Tartarus, and so are the rebellious angels in the Bible; Zeus rapes the daughters of man, and so do the "Sons of God" in Genesis 6; Ba'al demands worship, and so does Satan using the name of Ba'al Zebub in the Gospels; Hermes brings messages

---

13  Thus, I agree with C. S. Lewis, who says, "Of course I believe the composition, presentation and selection for inclusion in the Bible, of all the works to have been guided by the Holy Ghost. But I think He means us to have sacred myth & sacred fiction as well as sacred history." C. S. Lewis, *The Collected Letters of C. S. Lewis: Volume III; Narnia, Cambridge, and Joy 1950-1963*, ed. Walter Hooper (San Francisco: HarperSanFrancisco, 2007), 653.
14  Tolkien, "On Fairy-Stories," 71.
15  J. P. Moreland and William Lane Craig, *Philosophical Foundations for a Christian Worldview* (Downers Grove, IL: IVP, 2003), 490-499.

from the King of the Gods, and so does the angel Gabriel.

Of course, although all myths must have elements of the super-human, simply having the super-human doesn't make a particular narrative a myth. If the super-human is treated in a comical manner, for example, the narrative to which these characters belong becomes something less than myth; the characters and activities in a myth, says Tolkien, "must . . . be taken seriously, neither laughed at nor explained away."[16] This, incidentally, is probably why there is little humor in the Bible despite the fact that laughter is in and of itself good and one of God's proper titles, therefore, is the God of Laughter.[17] Thus, parodies of myths are just that—parodies, not myths—though of course myths do often contain a few light or comical moments within (I, for example, love the idea in Egyptian mythology that the Blessed-With-Ra will enjoy the "Beer of Everlastingness"!). Moreover, it is certainly possible that those who love a myth such as *Sleeping Beauty* might also love parodies of this myth, such as *Shrek*; but even so, such a person won't love these stories in the same way. Myths, then, are largely serious narratives concerning the greatest of subject matters, that is, the super-human. It is for this reason that Tolkien says, "Something really 'higher' is occasionally glimpsed in mythology: Divinity, the right to power, the due of worship; in fact 'religion.'"[18]

Hence, mythology has a deeply religious feel to it, which, furthermore, is proper to it. God wants us to make myths and myths are serious stories that concern, in large part, the super-natural or super-human. But is the religious sense of myth something to be *utterly* dissected as most philosophers of myth have argued? Some myths, perhaps: Ma'at in Egyptian mythology and Wisdom in the Bible, for instance, seem to be simply the Natural Law and Wisdom of God, and their feminine personalities seem completely unimportant. Nevertheless, is this also true of "Thor" and "thunder" or "Satan" and "evil"?

Again, Chesterton, Lewis and Tolkien all say no, and I agree with them. It is a false dilemma to see Hercules, a Greek demi-god, and Krishna, an avatar of the Hindu god Vishnu, as either metaphors for some higher truth or else "husk." In the best myths at least, the super-natural characters have personalities and are three-dimensional beings. Osiris, Ishtar, and Persephone are all dying-and-rising gods, and certainly in this sense are Christ-types; but they are also more than this. In their stories, they are persons in their own right, much the way that Mother Theresa maintains her humanity and "this-ness" even while reflecting Christ in her acts of charity. In *The Voyage of the*

---

16  Tolkien, "On Fairy-Stories," 54.
17  Nevertheless, there is probably more humor in the Bible than many non-Greek and non-Hebrew readers suspect. See Elton Truebold, *The Humor of Christ* (New York: Harper & Row, 1964).
18  Tolkien, "On Fairy-Stories," 25.

*Dawn Treader* when Eustace says a star "is a huge ball of flaming gas," he, in his hasty reductionism, fails to see that "that is not what a star is but only what it is made of."[19] Myths aren't allegories because in allegories particular personalities don't matter *at all*. One does well to remember that all of creation is a story—indeed, a myth—and creation isn't reducible to an allegory that God simply enjoys reflecting upon: God made real personalities, things and locations and delights in these in all their complexity. This is why myth can be seen as greater than allegory: while allegories give us a few important truths about reality, myths, when done well, give us a more well-rounded, complex vision of reality, that is, the reality of an enchanted creation brimming with human and super-human activity.

The metaphysical naturalist or a person who thinks that there is no such thing as a super-human realm might consider stories about super-human activity mere child's play—things to be enjoyed when in a state of naivety but certainly done away with when an adult. In fact, typically the naturalist will think that an adult who spends a lot of time dwelling on myth is hopelessly enslaved to wish-fulfillment, desiring an utterly unreal, meaningless state of affairs. But for the person who has good reason to think that there really are super-humans and that they interact with us, stories about the super-human in general won't simply be child's stuff, but will be *human* stuff; that is, they will concern us all, and, indeed, will have the power to awaken in us what Plato calls heavenly *eros*, the Romantics call *sehnsucht*, Lewis calls Joy, and the Christian tradition has often associated with hope, which is the rational desire for divine reality.[20] Moreover, myths, having a certain gravitas and religious

---

19  C. S. Lewis, *The Voyage of the Dawn Treader* (London: Fontana, 1984), 159.
20  Cf. "Finally, what shall we say about the stigma of 'escapism'? . . . Now there is a sense in which all reading whatsoever is an escape. . . . All such escape is *from* the same thing; immediate, concrete actuality. The important question is what we escape *to*. . . . Escape, then, is common to many good and bad kinds of reading. By adding –*ism* to it, we suggest, I suppose, a confirmed habit of escaping too often, or for too long, or into the wrong things, or using escape as a substitute for action where action is appropriate, and thus neglecting real opportunities and evading real obligations. If so, we must judge each case on its merits. Escape is not necessarily joined to escapism. The authors who lead us furthest into impossible regions—Sidney, Spenser, and Morris—were men active and stirring in the real world. The Renaissance and our own nineteenth century, periods prolific in literary fantasy, were periods of great energy. . . . Since the charge of escapism against a very unrealistic work is sometimes varied or reinforced with that of childishness . . . two points need to be made. . . . Most of the great fantasies and fairy-tales were not addressed to children at all, but to everyone. . . . Secondly, if we are to use the words *childish* or *infantile* as terms of disapproval, we must make sure that they refer only to those characteristics of childhood which we become better and happier by outgrowing; not to those which every sane man would keep if he could and which some are fortunate for keeping."

tone, are probably best enjoyed by adults, who, having more developed cognitive faculties than children, can better take in the profundity of myths. In this way, myths are not things to be transcended as we get older, but are to be carried with us into adulthood: they are ageless. Indeed, in the case of good myths, they are to be appreciated more, not less, as we get older just as a fine wine or cheese gets better with age, not worse. Myths are to be legitimate sources of emotional strength, drawing us up to a higher reality, not simply in childhood but also in our waning years. I myself enjoy both *Transformers: The Movie* (1984) and *Paradise Lost* more now as a 34-year old than I did as a 4- or 14-year old, which is what Lewis has in mind when he says that true growth is not exchanging one interest for another but adding new interests to old ones, as a tree adds new rings.

Nevertheless, some, even those who believe in the super-human realm, might still see mythology as kid's stuff because myths are not historically true: Marduk didn't really slay Tiamat, Aeneas didn't help found Rome and Izanami probably isn't still trapped in the Underworld. Of course, myth as myth—that is, myth separate from the question of historical truth—has many benefits: not only does it entertain, which in and of itself is good, but it also encourages us to think about super-natural reality, which, broadly speaking, is real and so, broadly speaking, is an edifying activity.

Nonetheless, there is something to the notion that historical truth adds value to myth. I myself am more fascinated with the Trojan War now knowing that Troy really existed than I was before, when I did not; and even knowing something about a real space agency like SETI (Search for Extra-Terrestrial Intelligence) makes my viewing of *X-Files* more thought-provoking, not less.[21] Furthermore, we have Lewis's important claim that Jesus is "the true myth"[22]—

---

C. S. Lewis, *An Experiment in Criticism* (Cambridge: Cambridge University Press, 1999), 68, 69, 70, 71.

21  Charles Taliaferro, *Aesthetics* (Oxford: Oneworld, 2011), 82.

22  "Now what Dyson and Tolkien showed me was this: that if I met the idea of sacrifice in a Pagan story I didn't mind it at all: again, that if I met the idea of a god sacrificing himself to himself . . . I liked it very much and was mysteriously moved by it: again, that the idea of the dying and reviving god (Balder, Adonis, Bacchus) similarly moved me provided that I met it anywhere *except* in the Gospels. The reason was that in Pagan stories I was prepared to feel the myth as profound and suggestive of meanings beyond my grasp even tho[ugh] I could not say in cold prose 'what it meant.' Now the story of Christ is simply a true myth: a myth working on us in the same way as the others, but with this tremendous difference that *it really happened*: and one must be content to accept it in the same way, remembering that it is God's myth where the others are men's myths: i.e. the Pagan stories are God expressing Himself through the minds of poets, using such images as He found there, while Christianity is God expressing Himself through what we call 'real things.' Therefore it is *true*, not in the sense of being a 'description' of God (that no finite mind could take in) but in

that Jesus fulfills in history what many pagans gods in their lives, deaths and resurrections achieved only in fiction. On this reading, Christ denounces, to be sure, many aspects of pagan myth—in one case, for example, He strongly distances Himself from Ba'al Zebub, who is associated with Satan; however, in another case, Christ, through His life, death and resurrection, can be seen to fulfill what the *Ba'al Cycle* in a vague way points at: that the hero god will die and then rise again. Christ's fulfillment of some major themes in non-historical mythology is thus similar to His fulfillment and perfection of the law and prophets of the Old Testament. Hence, non-historical myths relating to the dying-and-rising god, for example, are valuable independent of the question of how they reflect or allude to the great events of history; nonetheless, their value does increase because of what Christ, in history, has done.

In fact, I might be willing to go a bit further and argue that *all* the greatest myths have themes, such as the creation, the war between good and evil (including the war in Heaven), the Fall, the dying-and-rising god, the return of the king, the last battle and the slaying of the dragon, the final judgment, the destruction of evil, and the happy ending, which are especially affective precisely because they have, or will have, some exemplification in history. Both Joseph Campbell and J. R. R. Tolkien can be seen as saying something similar here. Campbell argues that the typical myth—including the best myths, I suppose—will (1) start in the ordinary, happy, humble world, but then a challenge will (2) be issued, which then, with great struggle, will (3) be overcome, ultimately resulting in a resurrection, reward or happy ending of some sort.[23] And Tolkien, for his part, says the greatest myths will (1) start with a happy creation which (2) gives way to a fall, where evil then overpowers the good only, when things are most dire, to (3) witness a "sudden joyous 'turn,'" in which the good returns with strength, resulting in a happy ending. For Tolkien, at least, this general theme of creation, fall and redemption so-to-speak is the stuff of myth, but is also the stuff of history. Speaking about the final movement of myth—the "eucatastrophe" or the return of good—Tolkien says, "It is the true form of the fairy-tale"—the "myth"—"and its highest function."[24] This is so because this movement—properly contextualized in

---

the sense of being the way in which God chooses to (or can) appear to our faculties. The 'doctrines' we get *out of* the true myth are of course *less* true: they are translations into our *concepts* and *ideas* of that wh[ich] God has already expressed in a language more adequate, namely the actual incarnation, crucifixion, and resurrection." Lewis, *The Collected Letters of C. S. Lewis: Volume I*, 996-997. Cf. "Our mythology is based on a solider reality than we dream." C. S. Lewis, *Perelandra*, in *The Cosmic Trilogy* by C. S. Lewis (London: Pan Books, 1990), 328.

23 Joseph Campbell and Bill Moyers, *The Power of Myth* (New York: Anchor, 1988), 304.

24 Tolkien, "On Fairy-Stories," 68.

the happy beginning and the dark middle—instantiates *evangelium*, calling to mind in very concrete, three-dimensional myths, from *The Odyssey* to *Star Wars*, the greatest theme of all, that of the Messiah, the Christ, the Hero.

So on my definition a myth is a concrete, serious, ageless, valuable narrative concerning super-humans who usually work out one or more of the great themes that has been or will be instantiated in history, and the more this narrative is in keeping with the aesthetic and moral good, which is grounded in God, the better it will be.

## SUPERHERO MYTHOLOGY

It is fairly commonplace nowadays for pop culture scholars to identify superhero narratives as mythology. Richard Reynolds, for example, does this in *Superheroes: A Modern Mythology* and Christopher Knowles, the author of *Our Gods Wear Spandex*, clearly identifies the serious, super-natural quality of superhero stories when he writes, "It was mythic heroes like The Mighty Thor, Doctor Strange and Captain America that most inspired me and instilled in me that vital sense of wonder. . . . It is precisely the reverential treatment of these characters—the essentially *religious* portrayal of them—that resonates with the mass audience today."[25] Comic book writers themselves have also increasingly started to see superhero stories in this light.[26] Thus, in *Justice League: Origin*, the members of the League are simply identified as "modern day gods,"[27] and in *Red Hulk: Mayan Rule*, Annie tells the Red Hulk after their

---

25  Christopher Knowles, *Our Gods Wear Spandex: The Secret History of Comic Book Heroes* (San Francisco: Weiser Books, 2007), xiv and 16. Also consider: "In a secular, scientific rational culture lacking in any convincing spiritual leadership, superhero stories speak loudly and boldly to our greatest fears, deepest longings, and highest aspirations. They're not afraid to be hopeful, not embarrassed to be optimistic, and utterly fearless in the dark. They're about as far from social realism as you can get, but the best superhero stories deal directly with mythic elements of human experience that we can all relate to, in ways that are imaginative, profound, funny and provocative. They exist to solve problems of all kinds and can always be counted on to find a way to save the day." Grant Morrison, *Supergods: What Masked Vigilantes, Miraculous Mutants, and a Sun God from Smallville Can Teach Us about Being Human* (New York: Spiegel & Grau, 2012), xvii.

26  This is not to say that early comic book writers like Stan Lee didn't *partially* see that what they were doing was making contemporary mythology, but rather it is to say that they weren't nearly as self-conscious of this as we might think. Indeed, in the case of Lee, he was surprised when an interviewer referred to his material as modern mythology, and Lee himself, even after this interview, appears to have thought of only his character Thor in these terms. See *Marvel Chronicle: A Year by Year History* (New York: DK, 2008), 88.

27  *Justice League: The Villains Journey*. In the introduction to *Kingdom Come*, Elliot Maggin also remarks, "This is the way we have always looked upon our super-heroes—

battle with the evil Mayan deities: "If any of the ancient Mayans were here to see all of the people we work with turning into animals, flying, shooting energy. Artificial men and women. What else would they call us? Face it, Giant Red Leader. In any age, we're what passes for gods. And our adventures are tomorrow's myths." Nevertheless, asserting that superhero narratives are myths is one thing, presenting evidence, and elaborating on this, is another.[28]

To begin with, few familiar with superhero stories will seriously doubt that these stories center around concrete, three-dimensional characters in concrete, three-dimensional worlds. True, some—many, even—early superhero adventures are fairly superficial, which is to say that the characterization and stories need a lot of work; Frank Miller, one of the world's most famous comic book writers, isn't completely wrong when he calls most of the early superhero stories "crap."[29] Nevertheless, superficiality isn't the same as allegory. J. Jonah Jameson, for example, is a fairly superficial *Spider-Man* character, yet he isn't simply "the boss" or the "comedic, deterring principle." He has a unique hair-cut, a wife who has a name, and a cigar-chomping-while-yelling habit that helps make him, him. And all of this particularity—not to mention the particularity of Peter Parker/Spider-Man, Aunt May, Norman Osborn and so on—help make *Spider-Man* stories, for example, concrete. Indeed, the sheer fact that most of the main superheroes have been around for decades, with hundreds of issues dedicated solely to them, makes it nearly inevitable that these heroes and their stories would be concrete things and thus potential myths.

Superhero narratives, moreover, are—at least since the mid-'80s—generally serious in tone. Certainly, these stories ask us to believe, literally speaking, that a man could really run around the world in a matter of minutes (the Flash), that Atlantis exists (Aquaman) and that a woman could possess the power of an alien entity (Ms. Marvel). And if the art and story are successful, we will believe in these secondary worlds; and if not, we won't. But either way, we are asked to believe in these worlds and not to treat the whole thing as comedy. Of course, some of the early superhero adventures aren't particularly serious, and there are a few explicit parodies of superhero adventures such as the '60s *Batman* TV series; nevertheless, most superhero stories are serious narratives, and in their seriousness, become potential myths.

---

as though they were gods."
28 Terrence Wadtke rightly denounces some studies which don't feel the need to elaborate on the "overly simple claim . . . that superhero stories resemble mythic stories of the past." Terrence Wandtke, *The Meaning of Superhero Comic Books* (Jefferson, NC: McFarland, 2012), 4.
29 Milo George, *Frank Miller: The Interviews, 1981-2003* (Seattle: Fantagraphics, 2003), 39.

## CHRISTIAN PHILOSOPHY AND SUPERHERO MYTHOLOGY

Furthermore, most superhero narratives are about *super-humans*. Indeed, most superheroes—and not just the ones plundered directly from mythology like Thor and Hercules—are themselves super-human. Even *Batman* stories are about the super-human, not simply because of the super-powered heroes or villains who make cameos in them, but also because Batman himself, despite being a human, isn't, as Lex Luthor says, "a mere mortal."[30] This is to say that Batman has a collection of abilities that no ordinary human being could ever possibly acquire, and the same is true for Robin, Batgirl and others like them. In this way, the cavemen that Bruce Wayne met when he was sent to the distant past weren't totally wrong to see him as "a god,"[31] and Robin was right to say of his thought-deceased mentor, "He was holy. He never gave up. No matter what. And over and over again, he'd pull off miracles. And finally he died for us. So I learned to do the impossible well."[32]

**ABOVE: ON THE LEFT, THOR, A DIVINE DRAGON SLAYER IN *FEAR ITSELF*, IS OBVIOUSLY SUPER-HUMAN, BUT SO, ARGUABLY, ARE BATMAN, ROBIN AND BATGIRL IN *THE BATMAN* (ON THE RIGHT) SINCE THEY POSSESS ABILITIES THAT NO ACTUAL HUMAN COULD POSSESS.**

Finally, even a brief encounter with superhero narratives is enough to reveal the presence of many, if not all, of the great mythic themes. For the sake of brevity, I'll consider just three of these: the gods in Heaven, the devils in Hell, and the battle between good and evil.

As for the gods in Heaven, God Himself (with a capital "G") is actually a character in both the DC and Marvel universes.[33] In the DC universe,

---

30  *Superman: The Animated Series* season 1, episode 9.
31  *Batman: The Return of Bruce Wayne.*
32  *Batman: Whatever Happened to the Caped Crusader?*
33  Batman, the Atom, Spider-Man, Wonder Woman, Green Lantern, the Huntress, Daredevil, Supergirl, the Fantastic Four, Beast and others all talk to and/or receive signs from God at one time or another, and the Sentry—one of the most powerful figures in the Marvel universe—is shown in *Dark Avengers Omnibus* to be possessed by the Void, which is the same power-spirit that filled Moses. Despite

for example, Batman accepts the *kalam* cosmological argument—that an Uncaused Cause exists—and though initially doubtful whether this Cause is the "bearded Creator sitting on His throne," the Caped Crusader receives an answer to prayer—a miracle—when he, in a moment of powerlessness, prays to this Cause for rain.[34] Indeed, later on in *Day of Judgment*, many of the major DC characters like Wonder Woman and Supergirl actually journey to Heaven, where they meet the angel Michael, the chief servant of God or "The Presence." Likewise, in the Marvel universe, Daredevil, though occasionally doubtful of God (once adding to his prayers, "if you even exist"), does continue to believe in, and pray to, God and, perhaps more importantly, continues to see his heroics as doing his "Father's work."[35] Additionally, many other major Marvel characters even meet God face-to-face, for example, Spider-Man on Earth, and the Fantastic Four in Heaven.[36] The existence of God Himself in superhero mythology is striking since as I pointed out earlier God is rarely explicitly present in non-biblical myths, even non-biblical myths by famous Christians such as Tolkien. As one might expect, I explore this notion further in this book, especially in chapters five and seven.

Of course, it's not just God who is in Heaven, but also the superheroes themselves, who, in a more limited sense, are often depicted as gods dwelling above us. For instance, the Justice League has their base of operations literally in the heavens—on the moon; and in Grant Morrison's run on *JLA*, he explicitly links this idea of a moon base with Mount Olympus, depicting Superman as Zeus, Wonder Woman as Hera, Batman as Hades, the Flash as Hermes, Green Lantern as Apollo, Aquaman as Neptune, and Plastic Man as Dionysius.[37] And this just scratches the surface. Superman, for example, has not only been compared to Zeus, but also to Hercules (in *All-Star Superman*), and, most importantly and most consistently, to Christ, which is a theme I elaborate on in chapter three of this book. Truly, "In Superman's world,

---

all this, arguably the most devote superhero in either the DC or Marvel universe is the X-Men's Nightcrawler. For example, in one episode of the *X-Men: The Animated Series*, Nightcrawler meets his long lost mother, Mystique, who abandoned him and betrayed him countless times. Nevertheless, citing God's forgiveness as his model, Nightcrawler forgives her and, in fact, risks his life to save her. *X-Men: The Animated Series* season 5, episode 6.

34 *Batman: Absolution*. Of course, Batman isn't always—isn't even typically—depicted as explicitly religious. For example, in *Batman: Whatever Happened to the Caped Crusader?* Batman is a more skeptical figure.

35 *Daredevil: Guardian Devil*. Concerning her son, Daredevil's mother prays, "He will be as a spear of lightning in your hand, My Lord." *Daredevil: Born Again*.

36 See chapter five of this book for details.

37 Morrison, *Supergods*, 292.

## CHRISTIAN PHILOSOPHY AND SUPERHERO MYTHOLOGY

everything is mythology."[38] Yet it's not just Superman but many—perhaps most—superheroes who are depicted in heavenly terms. In *Planet Hulk*, for example, the Hulk is portrayed as an alien savior-king who comes to a world not his own to help free an enslaved people, and in *Green Lantern* stories, the Guardians—who I discuss at greater length in chapter four of this book—dwell in distant space and are considered immortal.

As for Hell or the Underworld, it is a real place in both the DC and Marvel universes. In DC comic books like *Reign in Hell*, *JLA: New Maps of Hell* and *Underworld Unleashed*, Hell is shown to be a place of torment, occupied by the damned, including the Devil himself (called "Neron," a play on "666" from the Bible[39]). And even hellish places like the Phantom Zone have a mythical quality about them. For instance, C. S. Lewis's notion that Hell is a place "locked from the inside,"[40] is echoed in *Superman: For Tomorrow* when the Man of Steel comes to the realization that "What doesn't want to be saved, can't be." Hell is shown to be a destination chosen, and many—even many aliens, according to Martian Manhunter—choose it.[41]

However, even more interestingly is how in the Marvel universe Hell is sometimes connected with secular or naturalistic mythology. In *Journey into Mystery: The Manchester Gods*, new gods—"gods of industry," "gods of modernity," "gods of the modern age"—arrive on the scene in the form of living cities and trains. This in itself is a brilliant commentary on the naturalistic or materialistic worldview, showing that far from being deity-less, naturalistic philosophies have simply substituted one great super-human thing (technology or unguided evolution[42]) for another (God). What's more, these gods of industry are shown to be the unconscious slaves of the great fire demon of Norse mythology, Surtur, who manipulates the gods of the modern age into implementing his agenda of "doom."

Additionally, some superheroes like Captain Marvel and Wolverine actually go to Hell, though these persons are shown not to belong there. In *Wolverine Goes to Hell*, for example, Wolverine does recognize that he's

---

38   *Batman: Time and the Batman*.
39   Although the finer points of theology are often unsatisfactory in superhero mythology, sometimes they do get it right. For example, in *Day of Judgment* we are correctly told, "The wrath of Neron [the Devil] pales to God's hand of judgment."
40   C. S. Lewis, *The Problem of Pain*, in *Selected Books* [Long Edition] (London: HarperCollins, 1999), 538.
41   *JLA: New Maps of Hell*.
42   C. S. Lewis brilliantly explains the naturalistic myth of unguided evolution in "The Funeral of a Great Myth." Lewis argues that though this myth is certainly false, it is still good myth insofar as it is a heroic story of nothing becoming something. It is the story of a lowly atom overcoming massive obstacles and astronomical improbabilities, eventually to triumph and become man, the ruler of the cosmos.

## IMITATING THE SAINTS

an imperfect man ("I deserve this," he says at one point), and yet in Hell, Wolverine immediately finds himself, as a good man, opposed to the Devil, who subsequently crucifies Wolverine on an x-shaped cross or a *crux decussata*. Here we see not only the mythical notion of devils in Hell, but also the hero who descends into Hell to battle the great foe. Wolverine, indeed, is one of many superhero Christ-types.[43]

ABOVE: ON THE LEFT, BATMAN SEEKS PROTECTION UNDER THE BLOOD AND THE CROSS IN *BATMAN & DRACULA: RED RAIN*; IN THE CENTER, THE ORIGINAL GREEN LANTERN, ALAN SCOTT, HAS A MYTHICAL MOMENT WHEN HE MEETS THE ANGEL MICHAEL IN *DAY OF JUDGMENT*; AND ON THE RIGHT, WOLVERINE DESCENDS INTO HELL AND IS CRUCIFIED BY THE DEVIL IN *WOLVERINE GOES TO HELL*.

And this leads to the great mythic theme of the battle between good and evil, and, connected to this, the idea of the mythic hero.

Now although not all myths have a clear sense of good and evil, and although not all myths have an obvious, and certainly not a universally agreed upon, protagonist, most, and according to Tolkien, all the best, ones do. And I agree with him. The hero twins of Mayan mythology, Hunahpu and Xbalanque, are the central figures in their stories and were looked upon favorably by the ancient Mayans; nevertheless, while these heroes certainly demonstrate some universally admirable qualities, such as piety toward their father (the future Maize God), they are far from possessing all, or even most, of the moral virtues. In fact, besides their piety toward their father, they have

---

43  Since the time of Christ, the cross has become, among other things, a symbol of a just person being unjustly punished. Even the Japanese, one of the world's least Christian people, know this; thus in season 1, episode 10 of *X-Men: Anime*, the X-Men are captured by an enemy and, like Wolverine in *Wolverine Goes to Hell*, are made to hang on x-shaped crosses. Even original Japanese superheroes like Sailor Moon and the Sailor Scouts are shown hanging from crosses in *Sailor Moon R* season 2, episode 28.

few commendable qualities. Thus, on Tolkien's account of myth, with which I agree, a myth like that of the hero twins is a lesser myth, and its heroes, lesser heroes. Indeed, in any culture where justice is largely treated as a social construct or that which only benefits the group, the culture's myths will usually be poor, and their heroes, mere protagonists.

So what kind of morality do we find in superhero narratives, and how is the word "hero" understood? Within a decade of the first appearance of superhero narratives, a number of social commentators, from journalists to psychologists, began asking whether comic book stories, including superhero stories, are morally detrimental. Harriet Lee, for example, argued that comics in general weren't "spiritually uplifting,"[44] and Fredric Wertham, the notorious comic censor, thought that comic book stories glorified crime, disrespected authority, encouraged cruelty, promoted sexual liberality, and were an important factor in juvenile delinquency. Although Wertham was mostly opposed to horror and crime comic books, he did go so far as to claim that *Superman* stories, for example, encourage "phantasies of sadistic joy in seeing other people punished over and over again while you yourself remain immune."[45] Wertham's attack on comic books and superhero narratives led to the infamous Comics Code, which heavily censored the types of stories that comic books could tell, leaving the nation, if not divided, at least a bit confused about the kind of morality communicated in superhero narratives.

While Wertham is right that many horror and crime comic books of the '40s and '50s (not to mention nowadays) were excessive and probably inappropriate for young children, he makes two fundamental mistakes.

First, he wrongly assumes that comic books are purely for children. Insofar as most of the stories told in comic books can be called myths, they were, and are, intended to be enjoyed by both children and adults, and we know that one of the largest consumers of superhero stories during the war years, for example, were not children but American soldiers. Certainly nowadays, young adults and adults—those who have disposable income—read more comic books than children, and children get their superhero exposure mostly through TV, movies and toys.

Second, Wertham, who probably hadn't read many superhero comic books, failed to see that the enjoyment that children get from the violence in *Superman* comic books, for example, shouldn't be understood in most cases as a perverse power fantasy about seeing people get hurt—as if these books were the second coming of the Roman gladiatorial games—but rather this enjoyment should be seen as the child quite properly celebrating justice (treating each as

---

44 Amy Kiste Nyberg, *Seal of Approval: The History of the Comics Code* (Jackson, MISS: University Press of Mississippi, 1998), 13.
45 Ibid., 60.

it ought to be treated) and a great mythical theme (the triumph of good over evil). G. K. Chesterton once said that children like seeing villains punished in fairy tales because they love justice, while adults like seeing villains shown mercy because they themselves are wicked and need forgiveness. Perhaps, some of this applies to *Superman* adventures: ethically and mythically speaking, children—and not just children, of course, but adults as well—quite rightly enjoy seeing both good triumph over evil, and evil punished. This is not to say that superhero stories shouldn't depict mercy and forgiveness; rather, since mercy and forgiveness perfect justice, not contradict or do away with it, myths do well to make justice its first ethical concern—a theme that is further explored in both chapters one and three of this book.

Consequently, I would argue that superhero narratives are not only not, for the most part, catalysts of immorality, but rather are powerful allies of the moral good.[46] Indeed, I would go further and claim that outside of biblical myth, superhero myths are the most moral myths man has ever told, and, though this is not all that matters for determining good myth, the clear morality in many or most superhero stories make them among the best myths the world has yet heard. The evidence for this is as follows.

Our word "hero" comes from the Greek word *heros*, which means "great warrior," implying, truly, that heroes should have courage. Yet as a product of American culture in the twentieth century, the "hero" in "superhero" is very much a Christian idea. Of course, I'm the first to agree that Christ didn't come to teach us a new ethic so much as to redeem us; that is, I certainly agree that we can find in pre-Christian cultures across the globe not only basic principles of justice (general beneficence, special beneficence, piety, duties of the strong to the weak, etc.) but also the idea of sacrificial love, which, as I said before, perfects justice. Pagan Greeks as well as Christian Greeks knew that courage is admirable. Nevertheless, because pre-Christian cultures had to piece moral principles together on their own, and because these cultures, even the best of them, were fallen, the heroes they created for their myths were, even in the best of cases, lacking. This stands in contrast to the cultures that have grown up in the light of Christian teaching, for these cultures, including twentieth century American culture, have Christ as an exemplar of the perfectly moral man, and—because this perfectly moral man did more for others than anyone could ever do—these cultures have the model of the perfect hero.

Thus, in contrast to the thesis of Jewett and Lawrence, who see the

---

46 Cf. "I believe that a somewhat moralist approach to the superhero genre is warranted, given the nature of the superhero narrative. . . . Since superhero stories make morals their business, it is useful to respond by analyzing the morals from a 'moralist' perspective and judge these stories, at least to a degree, on their own terms." Marc DiPaolo, *War, Politics and Superheroes: Ethics and Propaganda in Comics and Film* (Jefferson, NC: McFarland, 2011), 5.

American superhero as nothing more than a lawless cowboy,[47] my argument is that the American superhero[48] is actually consciously or unconsciously modeled after Christ. And just as the battle between good and evil is clear in the stories of Christ, so too is the battle between good and evil in most superhero stories. In *The New Avengers Omnibus* vol. 1, Captain America asks Daredevil to join the New Avengers, but Daredevil, who is in the hot-seat, replies, "Even if Jesus Himself came back and joined the team . . . the next day all of you would be sucked under a bus just for knowing me." Although a joke, it's telling that the Avengers see Jesus as a person who, in many respects, would fit well with their vision and mission. Thus, acknowledging the obvious non-moral similarities between Christ and the superhero—that is, their super-human abilities—the Christ-type hero, and thus the ideal superhero, has at least four moral qualities that make him or her stand out.

First, the Christ-type hero is a competent, morally self-actualized, virtuous individual. In the Gospels, Christ is an orphan of a sort, and the same is true for many of our major superheroes like Peter Parker, Clark Kent and Bruce Wayne. Mythically speaking, the absence of one's parents often forces the potential hero in question to mature more quickly, meaning, for our purposes, that they can be seen as men on their own right or persons who are able to handle the heroic task looming in front of them. Yet even if not an orphan, the hero isn't someone who is born heroic or who without effort acts heroically; he or she needs time to develop—to grow in "wisdom and stature" as the Gospels say.[49] Jesus, after all, didn't begin his heroic mission until He was thirty. Thus, Batman is right when he says, "Being chosen doesn't make you a hero. What you choose does."[50]

---

47 John Shelton Lawrence and Robert Jewett, *The Myth of the American Superhero* (Grand Rapids, MI: Eerdmans, 2002). If we were to understand the cowboy as a lone figure who acts outside of the law, often to promote some moral good, then the cowboy ideal, one could easily argue, is actually just one component of the Christ-type since Christ himself embodied and did, to some extent, all of this.

48 Insofar as people are beings able to grasp universal concepts, both ethical and mythical ones, and insofar as Christ embodies and perfects these concepts, we should expect that Christ would have the potential to appeal to all people. And insofar as superheroes are modeled after Christ, they, too, should have such universal appeal. Some cultural relativists, of course, have argued that the superhero—as a figure that comes out of American culture—only appeals to Americans. But what they fail to see is that just because the superhero comes out of American culture, the superhero himself derives from a much more universal origin. Certainly judging from both domestic and international box office receipts of recent superhero films, superheroes have a massive global appeal.

49 Luke 2:52.

50 *Batman: The Brave and the Bold* season 1, episode 7.

Second, the Christ-type hero is, in contrast with nearly every ancient hero, humble. Christ, we are told, shed His glory to become a man who, in His hour of greatest anguish, was utterly abandoned. True, Christ's coming to Earth eventually gives Him glory, but the glory that Christ receives is not that of a tyrant who would surround himself with yes-men, or a being who desired the Fall only so that he could step in, save the day, and thus feel good about himself. Rather, the glory of Christ is the glory a son feels when he has pleased his father, or the glory a father feels when his son has done well. Many times in the Gospels Christ instructs people not to tell others who He is—not to tell others that He is the Messiah or Hero. There would be a time for that, but Christ was not hungry for that; He didn't desire the superficial glory that comes from being called a hero. And the same is true for most superheroes. Superhero myths make great efforts to show their heroes to be humble, and one of the ways they do this is through the notion of a secret identity.[51] Superman, Spider-Man and Batman save the day, to be sure, but Clark Kent, Peter Parker and Bruce Wayne never get the praise; indeed, these three are often ridiculed as bumbling, incompetent or superficial. Yet even so, the superhero maintains his secret identity because he prefers his family's safety[52] over lip-service: "A true hero," Spider-Man J says, "finishes the fight, but doesn't stick around for the glory!"[53] And this, incidentally, is what makes Superman, Spider-Man and Batman greater superheroes than others like Iron Man, for instance.[54]

Third, the Christ-type hero is passionate about justice or righteousness. While this isn't utterly unique to the Christ-type hero, Christians believe that Christ is the man who lived a perfectly just or righteous life. His very dying on the cross is evidence of His desire to pay the outstanding debt of injustice that man had committed against God, which must be paid in order to make possible the restoration of the relationship between God and sinful man. Superheroes, of course, are great lovers of justice; the sentiment in King David's "Oh how I love your law!"[55] is echoed in Cable's "only warped minds

---

51 Some gods in world mythologies disguise themselves while on Earth, but typically their motivation isn't humility or justice, but rather something more whimsical or even immoral. Zeus, for example, takes many different forms when on Earth, but he does so in order to commit adultery away from the jealous eyes of Hera, his wife.
52 As Elongated Man says, "Anyone who puts on a costume paints a bull's-eye on his family's chest." *Identity Crisis*.
53 *Spider-Man J: Japanese Knights*.
54 Many of the Marvel superheroes were intentionally designed with some minor moral flaws as a way to humanize them. This it did, but the consequence is that this also made them less mythic. The DC character Superman, for example, is the most perfect of all the superheroes and in this is also the most mythic.
55 Psalm 119:97.

## Christian Philosophy and Superhero Mythology

appreciate anything which violates the laws of Nature."⁵⁶ This is to say that true superheroes, as with Christ Himself, are moral realists—they believe in the Natural Law or in universal moral principles, both general and absolute—and stand by their principles.⁵⁷ They, of course, realize that there are many difficult moral dilemmas that require wisdom to negotiate and some superheroes do this better than others;⁵⁸ nevertheless, they reject the relativistic reasoning of super-villains, and plant their feet firmly against utilitarian arguments that would see the end justify whatever means required.⁵⁹ Thus, Captain America won't allow the evil Enchantress to kill the evil Baron Zemo, endorsing murder (the mean) in order to rid the world of a great evil (the end);⁶⁰ Superman won't kill an innocent woman (the mean) in order to stop the world-threatening demon possessing her (the end);⁶¹ Mister Fantastic won't let Galactus die (the mean) to prevent the possible destruction of countless worlds (the end);⁶² *Watchmen*'s Rorschach vows to expose Ozymandias's agenda of murdering millions (the mean) to save billions (the end);⁶³ and Batman won't allow Karan's bodyguard to murder Gotham's super-villains (the mean) even though the world would be better off without them (the end); thus, the Caped Crusader says it well when he remarks, "The code we [superheroes] work by isn't always the easiest way, but it is the right way."⁶⁴ And, of course, the justice that these heroes seek

---

56   *X-Men: The Complete Onslaught Epic* vol. 2.
57   Indeed, Superman explicitly accepts "Natural Law" in *Superman: Grounded* vol. 2.
58   Although so-called antiheroes like Magog, the Punisher and Ghost Rider appear to be straight-up utilitarians and thus not true Christ-type heroes, it's possible—though I wouldn't want to be the one to make the case—that a person could argue that while both Magog and Superman, for example, might agree with a universal principle of justice such as "It's always wrong to murder," they might still disagree about particular applications of justice and particular instances of apparent murder. Superman, one might argue, thinks that killing the Joker in cold blood is unjust killing (murder) whereas Magog thinks it just killing. *Justice Society of America: Thy Kingdom Come* vol. 3.
59   Thus, the Watcher tells the villain Apocalypse, "You must respect them [the superheroes]. For despite their sacrifice, they were unwilling to become like you and allow the end to justify any means." *X-Men: The Complete Onslaught Epic* vol. 2.
60   *The Avengers: Earth's Mightiest Heroes* season 2, episode 3. Or again, in *Avengers vs. X-Men*, Captain says, "If only the ends always justified the means."
61   Elliot Maggin, *Superman: Miracle Monday* (New York: Warner, 1981), 184.
62   *Fantastic Four: The Trial of Galactus*.
63   Thus, in *Watchmen*, Rorschach says, "There is good and there is evil, and evil must be punished. Even in the face of Armageddon I shall not compromise on this."
64   *The Batman* season 4, episode 10. Or again, in *Batman: The Killing Joke*, Commissioner Gordon, whose daughter was just shot by the Joker, tells Batman, "I want him brought in and I want him brought in by the book! . . . We have to show

is, as I elaborate more on in chapter one of this book, not so much against the laws of the land, so much as with-and-above them. Jesus tells us to obey the laws of the land ("Render unto Caesar what is Caesar's"[65]), yet in the name of truth and justice, doesn't hesitate to challenge the interpretations of the corrupt Jewish lawmakers; likewise, most superheroes work with their governments, sometimes going against them if they are corrupt, but mostly doing or completing the justice that the nation can't achieve on its own.[66]

Fourth, the Christ-type hero is a person of sacrificial or agape love. When Adam and Eve chose to sin against God, God was under no moral obligation to become incarnate, live a perfectly just life, die and rise again in order to restore them to fellowship with Himself. Insofar as we are like Adam and Eve—that is, free creatures who willingly choose injustice over justice—God is under no obligation to save us. Nevertheless, He, as the Christ, did pay the price of injustice Himself and thus is able to offer sinners the chance to be reconciled with Himself. All we have to do is truly speak justice ("I am a sinner; I can't save myself; God can") and we can be made whole. Christ's gracious offer of salvation to sinners is an act of sacrificial or agape love; it goes beyond the requirements of justice, but never, in the process, does it in anyway violate justice. Perhaps in this, more than in any other aspect of the hero, do we see the influence of Christ on the figure of the superhero. Yet even so, the agape sacrifice that superheroes make, as with the sacrifice of Christ, isn't a trivial one. True, giving a dollar or two to a person whom you have no obligation to give the money to is, or can be, agape, but strictly speaking this isn't what makes a hero, a hero. The hero's sacrifice—as with Christ's sacrifice—is greater; it means putting one's life on the line when one has no obligation to do so. Captain America, for example, risks his life to save many, including the villainess Madame Viper, adding, "I just wanted to set the world *right*, and she [Viper] needed to see that's what heroes do."[67] Wonder Woman understands the agape aspect of being a heroine when she says, "You don't deserve mercy, monster, but that's exactly why I'm granting it."[68] The same holds true for the Earth-2 Flash, who tells Gog, "You can't help people and demand something in return, Gog. That's not how it works."[69] Ditto for Hercules, who says, "You

---

him! We have to show him that our way works!"
65  Mark 12:17.
66  As Batman says again, "I believe in law, and in right and wrong." *Batman: Whatever Happened to the Caped Crusader?*
67  *Marvel Universe Avengers: Earth's Mightiest Heroes* vol. 2.
68  *Wonder Woman: Odyssey* vol. 2. In *Superman: Grounded* vol. 2, Wonder Woman, who was taught how to be a courageous pagan warrior but later became a Christ-type hero, says to Superman, "My sisters may have trained me to be a warrior, but you have shown me a glimmering of what it means to be a hero."
69  *Justice Society of America: Thy Kingdom Come* vol. 3.

call me the god of heroes? What heroes teach us is what the gods should be. . . . I do what any true god should do—what the heroes among us do every day. I give up everything to protect, to heal, to restore, and then to walk away."[70] And the list of examples goes on and on. Magneto tells Professor X that he can't save everyone, to which Professor X replies, "Remind me again; Later"— and then goes on trying to save those who need saving.[71] Or again, in *Crisis on Infinite Earths*, the Earth-3 Dr. Light says, "Tell me what to do and I'll sacrifice my own life if need be,"[72] and in *The Onslaught Epic*, we are told that "to defeat the greatest threat the world has known, the heroes were prepared to sacrifice themselves."[73] Consequently, I agree with Christopher Knowles when he claims, "All [true] superheroes are essentially savior figures."[74]

Bringing this all together, then, we might say that the true superhero is one who approximates to Christ, which is to say that he or she is a virtuous, law-abiding-but-not-law-restricted person who uses his or her super-human abilities in a competent and humble manner with the goal of bravely promoting justice and sacrificial love in a fairly significant way. And because the superhero is a mythical hero, and because the more moral the myth, the better, usually, the myth will be, superhero myths—which indeed I hope I have convinced you by now are in fact myths—are, or at least some of them are, among the greatest myths we have,[75] and thus are properly worthy of both our enjoyment and philosophical reflection.

This latter point, in fact, is the chief purpose of this book. All seven chapters, most of which were originally written as stand-alone essays, approach some aspect of superhero mythology through the lens of either explicit or implicit Christian philosophy. These chapters don't represent anything like an exhaustive study of superhero mythology, nor do they even deal with some of the most important themes or figures. Nevertheless, they should be of interest

---

70   *Chaos War*.
71   *X-Men: Age of Apocalypse Omnibus*.
72   *Crisis on Infinite Earths*.
73   *X-Men: The Complete Onslaught Epic* vol. 2.
74   Knowles, *Our Gods Wear Spandex*, 111. A milder and more general form of this statement is by Joseph Campbell, who says, "A hero is someone who has given his or her life to something bigger than oneself." Joseph Campbell and Bill Moyers, *The Power of Myth* (New York: Anchor, 1988), 304.
75   Although unable to give a philosophical argument why superhero myths are among the best myths in the world, Joe Quesada, the editor-in-chief of Marvel Comics, is right when he says, "Thanks to all the greats like Stan Lee . . . the foundation was set for what eventually became the greatest fantasy universe in the history of modern civilization. On par with the likes of Homer and Shakespeare, Stan and company gave us a litany of characters and fables not seen since the stories of the all-powerful Greek and Roman pantheon of deities." *Marvel Chronicle*, 342.

for those desiring to think harder about superhero mythology, and my hope is that this reflection will even lead some to personal ethical transformation and action. When St. Paul says, "Imitate me, as I imitate Christ," he gives us biblical justification for imitating the saints.[76] And so perhaps after reading through this book, you will find some room to agree that insofar as superheroes like Captain America are heroes modeled after Christ,[77] to imitate them is also, to some extent, to imitate Christ.[78]

---

76   1 Corinthians 11:1.
77   Concerning the recently deceased Captain America, we are told, "He was like that sainted, can-do-no-wrong big brother." *Captain America: The Death of Captain America; The Death of the Dream.*
78   In *Birds of Prey: Between Dark & Dawn*, the Huntress investigates the Second Heaven cult, in whose church they have a sainted glass window of Superman battling Darkseid, about which the Huntress comments, "I'm not too crazy about churches in general but that offends even me." If my argument in this introduction has been convincing, it should be clear that, properly understood (that is, not as idolatry but as saint-imitation), the Huntress shouldn't be particularly offended by this depiction. Cf. "In some places, we'll be following the old Christian tradition of studying 'exemplary lives. . . . The saints' lives themselves are really early stories of superheroes: through their faith, the saints often performed super-human physical and spiritual feats, bona fide miracles." Greg Garrett, *Holy Superheroes! Exploring the Sacred in Comics, Graphic Novels and Film* (Louisville, KY: Westminster John Knox, 2008), x.

# CHAPTER ONE

## The Political Legacy of Superheroes

Summer 2011 saw the release of the HBO documentary *Superheroes*, which filmed the exploits of fifty real-life, self-styled superheroes across North America. One such superhero, Thanatos, has patrolled Vancouver for four years, mostly handing out bottled water and blankets to the homeless, but, of course, always doing so while wearing his green skull mask to hide his true identity. Another, Benjamin Foder, a.k.a. Phoenix Jones, was recently forced to unmask after being arrested for using pepper spray to help break up a fight outside a Seattle nightclub.[1] What is clear from the documentary is while most, if not all, of these real-life superheroes have strong individual desires to promote public justice, they tend to see the political system, especially the police force, as broken, corrupt or compromised, and so, for the sake of moral integrity and symbolic purity, choose to work outside of it.[2] This, I shall argue, is the political legacy of their fictitious forefathers, the greatest superheroes of the DC and Marvel universes.

### SUPERMAN AND THE JUSTICE LEAGUE

The DC universe is older than the Marvel one, and so it's there that we must begin if we want to get at the roots of superhero non-partisanship.

At the center of the DC universe is the grandfather of all superheroes: Superman. Though originally the name of a bald villain bent on world domination (yep) and based loosely on Nietzsche's *übermensch* (a popular, though misleading symbol of German aggression during World War I), Superman was later completely re-envisioned by his co-creators, Jewish American cartoonists Jerry Siegel and Joe Shuster. The model for the re-envisioned Superman was himself a figure who had, at least the first time He was here in the flesh, no earthly political ambition at all: Jesus.[3]

---

1   Michael Woods, "Meet Thanatos, Polarman and Dark Guardian," *Toronto Star* Saturday, November 26, 2011.
2   During the Arab Spring revolts and subsequent unrest in Egypt, many women were heckled or harassed, but a group of young men—vigilantes—tried to stop this, doing things like spray painting harassers. They needed to this because the police, mostly corrupt, stood by and watched. *New York Times* Saturday, November 17, 2012.
3   For more on this, see chapter three of this book.

# Imitating the Saints

In *Action Comics* vol. 1, #1 Superman was sent from his home planet of Krypton to Earth and, on Earth, was raised by his virtuous adoptive parents, *Mary* and Jonathan *Joseph* Kent. Sometime later "Mary" was changed to "Martha," but the allusions to Superman as a Christ-type endured and expanded. In the early 1940s, Superman's real name was revealed to be Kal-El, where *el* is the Hebrew word meaning "of God" (as in either *El*ohim or Gabri*el*). At roughly the same time, his powers were explained to be caused by the Earth's yellow sun, a timeless metaphor for God Himself. In the 1978 *Superman: The Movie*, Superman's true father sends him to Earth, not so much to save his son this time, but rather to save earthlings; he tells him, "They can be a great people, Kal-El, if they wish to be. They only lack the light to show the way. For this reason, above all, their capacity for good, I have sent them you, my only son." And finally a decade later, DC had Superman die at the hands of Doomsday, only to have him return from the dead to defeat the anti-Superman, Hank Henshaw, and restore hope to the world once again.

Yet perhaps most relevant in all this is Superman's absolute moral integrity, symbolically reflected in his code against killing and lying. Like Jesus, Superman is depicted as being morally superior to all those around him, including those who are most expected to administer justice: the state and its coercive forces, the police and military. Where the world is broken, where "the world changed," the antihero Magog tells—accuses—Superman in *Kingdom Come*, "you wouldn't."[4] Although America's, and the World's, politics are constantly changing, and though what once appeared black and white has become grey, Superman, as a Christ-type, continues to see things clearly.[5]

Of course, some will say that Superman's color clarity is to see white as red, white and blue, and black as whoever stands opposed to America's politics. These will ask, doesn't his costume kind of look like the flag?[6] Doesn't he himself admit that he fights for "Truth, Justice and the American Way"? Isn't he an arch-Republican and conservative, the very symbol of American nationalistic arrogance?

These objections are commonly heard, but confuse patriotism for politics. Christians have typically maintained that we have a general moral duty to favor those closest to ourselves over others. For example, if there were two starving girls in front of me who were identical in every way save for the fact that one happened to be my daughter, and if I had only one indivisible unit of food to

---

4  *Kingdom Come*.
5  Of course, Superman himself doesn't pretend that things are always morally simple. As he says in *Superman: Grounded* vol. 2, "There may be a right and a wrong in the universe, but it isn't always easy to tell the difference."
6  In *Batman, The Dark Knight: Knight Terrors*, a poisoned Batman scorns Superman for wearing "the American flag."

distribute, then I would act rightly by giving it to my daughter and would act wrongly by giving it to the other girl. To give the food to the other girl out of agape love would be a violation of justice and hence wouldn't be agape love at all since love completes justice, never does away with it. The command to favor those closest to ourselves, of course, decreases in potency the further we move away from our families, but nevertheless probably remains in a very mild form when we get to the national level. Hence, patriotism is rightly considered a virtue, even if a minor one.[7] For example, we would rightly think a typical Canadian citizen somewhat flawed in character if he, for example, were to cheer for Team U. S. in the men's hockey gold medal game rather than for Team Canada. Thus, I think it somewhat apparent that loving one's country is a good thing—not as obviously good as bare truth and justice, but still a good thing—and that loving one's country entails neither approving of its policies nor thinking it can only be improved through political channels.

Subsequently, to fight for the "American Way" doesn't mean fighting in defense of America's foreign policies,[8] for example, though Superman did help the Allies fight the Axis powers during World War II. Superman, as one raised by an American family, naturally loves America and her way of life, and, all things being equal, quite properly defends her.[9] Nevertheless, because the "American Way" part of the phrase did, in the global popular imagination, become associated with aggressive Americanism across the planet, in the past decade the phrase has changed to see Superman fighting for "Truth, Justice and all that"[10] or "Truth, Justice and the Universal Way."[11] Even more significantly, in *Action Comics* vol. 1, #900, Superman gives up his American citizenship, not because he has stopped loving his country above all others (his costume still resembles the flag) but because too many American politicians want to use him to promote controversial American foreign policies. "I'm tired of having my actions construed as instruments of U. S. policy," he tells the Secretary to

---

7   Here I disagree with Alasdair MacIntyre, who argues that favoring one's country over another must be based on purely non-moral reasons. See Alasdair MacIntyre, *Is Patriotism a Virtue?* (Lawrence, KS: University Press of Kansas, 1984).
8   Most superheroes understand the distinction between patriotism and policy-approving, yet there are a few ignorant ones, like Dr. Mid-Nite, who is shocked to see a left-leaning superhero like Green Arrow tell Despero, "No one soils my country's flag." Dr. Mid-Nite is so surprised that he says to Green Arrow, "I didn't know you were a patriot," to which Green Arrow replies, "Hell, I bleed red, white and blue . . . just different shades than most of you." *JLA/JSA: Virtue and Vice.*
9   The "American Way" part of the phrase could be seen as Superman's love for America per se, but it could also be understood as Superman's strong support for "life, liberty and the pursuit of happiness." See *Superman: Grounded* vol. 2.
10  *Superman Returns*, directed by Bryan Singer (Warner Bros., 2006).
11  *The Brightest Day* vol. 2.

the President, "I'm an alien born on another world. I can't help but see the bigger picture." For Superman, as for us all hopefully, serving the interests of one's family and nation, though important moral considerations, shouldn't be the only, or even the primary, moral considerations.

As shocking as this all has been to some Americans, this was a long time coming. Superman and the entire Justice League of America (JLA) have worked outside the American judicial system from the beginning because while the American judicial system and military may (the key word here) be better than most in the world, they aren't ideal, and Superman, as a Christ-type, is supposed be an ideal. Wonder Woman, too, carries nothing less than the Lasso of Truth, which helps her overcome so much of the complexity that plagues real-life moral deliberation and politics. Batman works with, but also outside, the Gotham police force, not only because it is diseased, but also because as one outside the system, the Dark Knight can act, as he says in *Batman Begins*, as "a *symbol* to shake people out of their apathy." And finally Green Lantern, who belongs to the cosmic police force formed by the "omniscient" Guardians of the Universe,[12] is beyond national politics, again acting from a position of superior wisdom and power than those on Earth. The term "America" in the Justice League of America, in other words, is simply indicative of where the members live rather than its political association.

In fact, the JLA is nicely contrasted with the JLI (the Justice League International). The former is fully autonomous and almost perfectly wise and good, whereas the latter are the third-stringers of the DC universe, in effect, the stooges of the UN, who are shown to be manipulated by the world organization and forced to tow the party line on some issues that they may personally disagree with.[13]

Now don't get me wrong: both leagues would agree with St. Paul's political vision, insisting that all "submit to governing authorities"[14] insofar as these authorities are agents of justice—"to bring punishment on the wrongdoers"[15]—and not insofar as they are unjust (St. Paul himself refused to worship the emperor as a god and even escaped from, rather than submit to, the unjust King Aretas[16]). Nevertheless, while the JLA feels free to disagree and act against any point they deem to be morally unacceptable—and when Lex Luthor was president, there were many of these[17]—the JLI would, unless the injustice is tremendously serious, not be so free.

Lest we think Superman and the Justice League are tyrants, even well-

---

12 *Trinity*. For more on the Guardians, see chapter four of this book.
13 *Justice League International: Signal Masters*.
14 Romans 13:1. Cf. Titus 3:1.
15 Romans 4:1.
16 2 Corinthians 11:32-33.
17 *Superman: President Luthor*.

meaning tyrants like Plato's guardians, we must remember that in the DC universe, Superman and the League—the big guns of the DC universe—aren't supposed to be like the rest of us fallen humanity. Yes, Batman is dark and complex, but his judgment and morals never are. "Sure we're criminals," admits Batman in *The Dark Knight Returns*—but Bats and the rest of the League can only be considered criminals in the same way Jesus was considered a criminal under Jewish or Roman law. As the Joker says of the Caped Crusader, "You truly are incorruptible."[18] The members of the JLA are more divine than human, and this is why their political legacy is in fact a legacy of trans-, and not so much anti-, politics. Superman and the League are moral symbols, not political figures, but their moral excellence is part of their political legacy, for they continue to inspire citizens of the world, including politicians, to be better than they are. Thus, Superman, flying with outstretched arms next to Christ the Redeemer statue in Rio de Janeiro, says of global hunger, "It's not my place to dictate policy for humankind. But perhaps the sight of me fighting hunger on a global scale would inspire others to take action in their own way."[19]

## CAPTAIN AMERICA AND THE MARVEL UNIVERSE

When we turn from the DC universe to the Marvel one, the political legacy of the marquee superheroes is more nuanced—more human, we could say—yet the dominant trend is very much in step with the DC universe.

To begin with, there is the issue of public disclosure. While all of the major superheroes in the DC universe—Superman, Batman, Wonder Woman, the Flash and Green Lantern—are masked or hide their true identities, this is only partially true in the Marvel universe. Iron Man, Thor, most of the X-Men and the Fantastic Four—huge Marvel figures—are very open about their true identities, and the true identities of Captain America and the Hulk are known to the military. Of the big names in the Marvel universe, only Spider-Man is secretive.

Moreover, whereas no superhero in the DC universe openly supports a real-world politician, Marvel's Spider-Man, for example, was depicted shaking hands with Obama during the last American election,[20] which could

---

18 *The Dark Knight*, directed by Christopher Nolan (Warner Bros., 2008). In *Batman: Gotham Knight*, the Scarecrow kidnaps a priest and asks, just before he executes him, "Will anyone speak for the holy man?" to which the Caped Crusader replies, "I will." This is a beautiful reply since Batman not only saves the priest, showing his own holy character, but his words can also be understood to mean that Batman is himself holy since he can speak on behalf of the holy. *Batman: Gotham Knight*, directed by Toshi Hiruma et al. (Warner Home Video, 2008).
19 *Superman: Peace on Earth*.
20 *The Amazing Spider-Man: Election Day*.

be construed as partisanship, but which could also be simply a tribute to the President, who has openly admitted to being a huge *Spider-Man* fan.[21]

Of course, superhero political commentary is part of the superhero legacy in both the DC and Marvel universes: Superman and Wonder Woman, for instance, fight Nazis just as much as Captain America. But though few will admit that any war is straightforwardly good vs. evil, few would disagree that the Allies were right to wage war against Hitler and the Axis powers. In other words, we don't need to see Superman, Wonder Woman and Captain America as political figures per se, so much as moral figures who happened to side with the U. S. in this conflict because the U. S. happened to be in the right. And even though for a season the Comics Code would prevent Captain from denouncing particular actions done by the Americans during the war,[22] such as nuking Japan, he was eventually able to do so; thus, in *Daredevil: Born Again*, Captain America tells an American General, "We could have won the war with clean hands, not with millions of innocents murdered by atomic fire."

Indeed, in the latest *Captain America* movie (2011), this is made quite clear insofar as Steve Rogers is a man who passionately wants to join the American military during the Second World War, not because he wants to kill Nazis, but rather because he doesn't "like bullies." Rogers, a.k.a. Captain America, is selected to be the test subject for the Super-Solider project, not because he is a mindless worshipper of all things American military, but rather because he is more virtuous than the rest: as Dr. Abraham Erskine tells Rogers, "You must promise me that whatever happens, you will stay who you are. *Not a perfect solider, but a good man.*"

Though some see this movie as historical revisionism—an attempt to cover up Captain's embodiment of "pop fascism"[23]—this movie is actually very true to the original spirit of Captain America, who was outraged by the Nazi's unjust treatment of the Jews, and was depicted punching Hitler on the jaw even before the U. S. entered the war. If Captain America had anything to do with inspiring America to enter the war, it would have been by showing America

---

21  Marc DiPaolo, *War, Politics and Superheroes: Ethics and Propaganda in Comics and Film* (London: McFarland, 2011), 1.
22  Amy Kiste Nyberg, *Seal of Approval: The History of the Comics Code* (Jackson, MS: University Press of Mississippi, 1998), ix.
23  Robert Jewett and John Shelton Lawrence, *Captain America and the Crusade against Evil* (Grand Rapids, MI: Eerdmans, 2004), 29. Truth be told, Jewett and Lawrence sound more like the villain Dr. Faustus, who tries to convince Captain's friend Bucky that because there are "no true heroes," Captain America couldn't be a true hero. However, still being able to discern good and evil, Bucky replies, "You can't twist it around . . . not anymore . . . you can't make me think those guys [including Captain] were anything but heroes." *Captain America: The Death of Captain America; The Burden of Dreams.*

that Hitler was first and foremost a man with the wrong morals, rather than a man with the wrong policies. From the beginning, Captain America has represented America at her best or the "American Dream,"[24] which, above all, is a symbol of outstanding morality; thus, the ghost of Captain America tells Thor, "All my life I fought to become a symbol. A symbol of all the things that were right about this country, all the things I loved. . . . It was never about politics."[25] This is why when given the opportunity to run for the presidency, Captain turns it down—it really wasn't about the politics for him.[26]

Indeed, if Captain America's primary allegiance is still doubted, consider the Marvel comic event *Civil War*. During this event, the Marvel superhero community was divided over the Superhero Registration Act, which required all superheroes to unmask and register as American civil servants (with salaries, benefits and all). Not coincidently, this Act coincided with the Patriot Act, which limited citizen's rights to privacy in the name of national security. One group of superheroes, led by Iron Man, supported the act, and helped the government capture, and detain without trial (à la Guantanamo Bay), all those who opposed it. Mister Fantastic, of the Fantastic Four, was also on board, and, mirroring the second war in Iraq, led his team to Latvia, a foreign country once ruled by Dr. Doom, and "liberated" it, only to find that the natives resented his liberation and saw him as a tyrant on par with Doom himself.[27] And finally, Iron Man and the other registered superheroes even stooped as low as to recruit super-villains like the Green Goblin and Venom to help them hunt down unregistered criminals like Captain America, who led the opposition to the Registration Act, declaring the government's law unjust, and eventually going underground to lead the resistance, saying, "Superheroes need to stay above [politics] or Washington starts telling us who the super-villains are." Because Captain America is the moral light—the Superman—of the Marvel universe, it's clear in the comics that Captain was in the right. Thus, after the events of *Civil War* played out, Captain was vindicated, and the other pro-registration supporters, including Iron Man, Mister Fantastic and Spider-Man, all joined him in upholding the code of all the greatest superheroes: independence from government control.[28]

---

24 Thus, Captain says, "I'm loyal to nothing, General, except the [American] Dream." *Daredevil: Born Again*.
25 *Thor Omnibus* (2007).
26 *Captain America* vol. 2, #250 (June 1980).
27 *Fantastic Four: Authoritative Action*.
28 I say "greatest superheroes" since some minor superheroes or superhero teams have always worked under government control. Canada's superhero team, Alpha Flight, for example, is funded by the Canadian government. Yet even so, the team leader, Vindicator (whose uniform is a giant Canadian flag), says, "I never fought for the law. Or the flag. I fought for the people." *Alpha Flight: The Complete Collection*

# Imitating the Saints

ABOVE: BOTH CAPTAIN AMERICA IN *CIVIL WAR* (ON THE LEFT) AND SUPERMAN IN *SUPERMAN: THE MOVIE* (ON THE RIGHT) RIGHTLY RECOGNIZE THEY HAVE MORAL DUTIES TO THEIR COUNTRY, BUT THEY NEVER ELEVATE THESE DUTIES ABOVE GREATER MORAL CONSIDERATIONS.

## THE LEGACY

Although the political legacy of superheroes is worthy of an entire book, I hope that the general contours are clear. For the most part, the greatest of the superheroes—Superman in the DC universe and Captain America in the Marvel one—are great because they are symbols of moral integrity. Being so, their political legacy has been one that properly sees them loving their countries and working with their governments insofar as they can, but also boldly acting against the government where conscience requires it.

But this isn't all they are: superheroes aren't merely political activists like those of the Occupy Wall Street movement nor are they simply about helping the homeless or pepper spraying minor criminals as with Thanatos or Phoenix Jones. The Occupy protesters and the real-life superheroes lack two key qualities that the best of the DC and Marvel universes possess.

The first quality is power. Superheroes fight—not just with words or worldly weapons, but with wonders—against injustice. They fight in ways that ordinary men and governments, because of their corruption or limited abilities, are incapable of doing. The ancient Chinese emperors needed *te* in order to implement the Mandate of Heaven, and the prophets and disciples of old performed miracles—acts of power—to demonstrate the truth of their message. Superman has invulnerable skin; the Occupy protesters have tents. Wonder Woman has a magical lasso; Phoenix Jones, pepper spray. Captain America has an unbreakable shield; Thanatos has bottled water. In *The Dark Knight*, a Batman look-a-like asks the real Caped Crusader, "What's the difference between you and me?" to which Batman replies, "I'm not wearing hockey pads."

The second quality is moral perfection. While many are familiar with Aristotle's understanding of virtue and the virtuous man, few are familiar with

---

(2012).

his understanding of godlike excellence and the hero or the man who "seemed not the child of a mortal man, but as one that came of God's seed."[29] The reason, of course, for this ignorance is understandable: the Philosopher devoted no more than a paragraph to this superman. For Aristotle, the best a human being could ever realistically be is virtuous and magnanimous. Nevertheless, he never denied the notion of a true hero or superman, and perhaps if he could have traded places with Anna the prophetess, or even, *per impossibile*, the fictitious Lois Lane, he could have met one.

Sadly, we are Aristotles, not Annas, and so it's doubtful that we'll see any genuine superheroes in our lifetime. Nevertheless, the fact that we have men like Phoenix Jones and Thanatos walking the streets because they feel inspired to make the world—a broken world—a better place should stir in us admiration, not ridicule. The masks they wear "make them," in the words of Spider-Man, "stronger" because they inspire and ennoble the wearer. True, we might feel better if men like Phoenix Jones and Thanatos—fallen men, as we all are—worked to reform the system from within, but we might still be encouraged by their motives. The world, including the political world, needs, and always will need, heroes to motivate it to become more Christ-like than it is.[30]

---

29  Aristotle *Ethics* 1145a.
30  *The Amazing Spider-Man*, directed by Marc Webb (Columbia Pictures, 2012). Cf. "It should give us hope that superhero stories are flourishing everywhere because they are a bright flickering song of our need to move on, to imagine the better, more just, and more proactive people we can be." Grant Morrison, *Supergods: What Masked Vigilantes, Miraculous Mutants, and a Sun God from Smallville Can Teach Us about Being Human* (New York: Spiegel & Grau, 2012), 414.

# Imitating the Saints

# CHAPTER TWO

## GENDER, DISABILITY AND SUPERHEROES

Mythology is for everyone: Jew, gentile, slave, free, male and female are all called to its table. Indeed, the creation and enjoyment of mythology is proper to humans as humans. And while we should never imagine that the value and greatness of a myth rests in a myth equally representing persons of all particularities, it is one of the glories of superhero mythology that it does make some effort to include heroes of different genders, races, ages, and (dis)abilities. And while the topics of race and age, for instance, are very interesting and worthy of philosophical discussion, my focus in this chapter will be on gender and disabilities related to gender, in particular, homosexual orientation. What I want to explore is not only how these are portrayed in superhero mythology, but also how they *should be portrayed*—the greatness of, and the benefit we receive from, myth increasing with its proximity to the good, which is best understood from an orthodox Christian perspective. Because the topic of sexual orientation is only properly understood in the light of a correct understanding of the nature of, and duties that flow out of, gender, I begin with the nature of gender.

## THE NATURE OF GENDER

God is a character in both the DC and Marvel universes.[1] And while we only know a few things about Him in these universes, we can gather that He is supposed to be the omniscient, omnipotent, loving Creator, and in these respects reflects the orthodox Christian understanding. But what about DC and Marvel depictions of God's gender? We can only say what is shown, but when God is shown, He is always depicted as masculine. And this also agrees with the orthodox Christian understanding of God, which I think is worth spending a few minutes unpacking.

---

1   For more on this, see chapter five of this book.

ABOVE: *Peter Parker, Spider-Man: Back in Black* (on the left) and *Fantastic Four: Hereafter* (on the right) both agree with orthodox Christianity in depicting God as masculine.

Propositions are either true or false, yet because humans aren't omniscient, we might not know whether a given proposition is either true or false. When we try to understand the nature of God, there will always be propositions whose truth we can't grasp as we now stand—propositions expressing what theologians call "mysteries." Nevertheless, orthodox Christians generally agree that we can know, to some extent at least, the truth and falsity of some propositions about God—that because of God's revelation to us, we can speak with some univocity about some aspects of Him. For instance, in both superhero mythology and the Bible, God is called Love, indeed, Sacrificial Love. From an orthodox Christian perspective, the biblical proposition "God is Love" is more literally and more precisely taken to mean, "God is the Being-Who-Most-Perfectly-Sacrifices-For-Others," and this, moreover, is taken to be *true*. Orthodox Christians think not only that God exists, but also that He is the essentially sacrificial being.

While some Christian feminists agree that propositions expressing God's omnipotence, omniscience and love are true, most deny that propositions expressing God's gender are. "Father," "King," "God," "husband," "she-bear," "mother hen," and so on are metaphors, the literal truth behind these words, and the propositions expressing these words, being something like "powerful," "leader-like," or "caring." "God is powerful" is true, but "God is King" is not; "God is caring" is true, but "God is a mother hen" is not. The metaphysical assumption behind Christian feminism, and feminism in general, is that gender is a social construct—a purely man-made thing, and thus, ever-changing. Consequently, all words and propositions expressing gender, especially in respect to God, are taken non-literally.

Yet the social construct thesis of feminism is much more at home in modern reductionistic philosophies than in orthodox Christianity. Certainly the Bible speaks of God as gendered, and, with almost perfect consistency, depicts Him as masculine. For example, Jesus teaches us to pray, "Our *Father* in Heaven," which could certainly also mean "Our Originator" and "Our

Parent," yet neither of these generic terms by themselves fully get at the meaning of "Father." Even more to the point, if we were to substitute "Mother" here instead of "Father," would this prayer not only mean less than before (as with "Originator" or "Parent") but also, unlike with "Originator" or "Parent," have, in fact, a diverging meaning? Would something not simply be lost but also distorted? Are mothers as mothers the same as parents as parents and are these exactly the same as fathers as fathers? Surely not; fathers as fathers have a kind of benevolent authority that mothers as mothers don't, and can't, have, and because parents include both fathers and mothers, parents, though a term closer to father than mother, is still incomplete. As C. S. Lewis writes,

> Suppose the reformer stops saying that a good woman may be like God and begins saying that God is like a good woman. Suppose he says that we might just as well pray to 'Our Mother which art in Heaven' as to 'Our Father.' Suppose he suggests that the Incarnation might just as well have taken a female as a male form, and the Second Person of the Trinity be as well called the Daughter as the Son. Suppose, finally, that the mystical marriage were reversed, that the Church were the Bridegroom and Christ the Bride. Now it is surely the case that if all these supposals were ever carried into effect we should be embarked on a different religion. Goddesses have, of course, been worshipped: many religions have had priestesses. But they are religions quite different in character from Christianity. Common sense, disregarding the discomfort, or even the horror, which the idea of turning all our theological language into the feminine gender arouses in most Christians, will ask 'Why not?' Since God is in fact not a biological being and has no sex, what can it matter whether we say *He* or *She, Father* or *Mother, Son* or *Daughter*? But Christians think that God Himself has taught us how to speak of Him. To say that it does not matter is to say either that all the masculine imagery is not inspired, is merely human in origin, or else that, though inspired, it is quite arbitrary and unessential. And this is surely intolerable: or, if tolerable, it is an argument not in favor of Christian priestesses but against Christianity. It is also surely based on a shallow view of imagery.[2]

Now certainly some terms used to describe God are best understood as metaphors—"mother hen," for instance—yet others are probably best understood more literally, and all the gender terms that are best understood literally are, according to theologian John Cooper, masculine ones. In line with Christian orthodoxy, Cooper says words like "Father," "King'" and "God'"—

---

[2] C. S. Lewis, "Priestesses in the Church?" in *C. S. Lewis: Essay Collection and Other Short Pieces*, ed. Lesley Walmsley (London: HarperCollins, 2000), 400-401.

words depicting prime masculinity—are "title-names"[3] or terms literally true of God, while others like "husband" and "bridegroom" are metaphors (though probably based on God being literally masculine). C. S. Lewis further argues that the biblical vision is one where "Gender is a more fundamental reality than sex,"[4] and if Cooper and Lewis are right—and I think they are—then one could argue that the true biblical vision of God in respect to gender is that of the Prime Masculine.

Without getting into too many details, the metaphysics of this would probably require two things. First, we'd need to agree that God is, as the Bible and most Christian philosophers argue, a "spirit," which, in Aristotelian language, is a (rational) soul, substance (as in, "Three persons in one substance"), or an indivisible whole with a number of essential properties (qualities or attributes that are *necessarily* part of that substance). Second, we'd need to agree that insofar as the Bible seems to assert the truth of propositions literally describing God as King, Father and God, that God has the property, indeed, the essential property, of "being masculine."

Of course, to avoid this type of gender essentialism, most feminists abandon essentialism altogether, a move which produces countless serious metaphysical problems in and of itself. Yet let's say for the sake of argument that some feminists are gender essentialists, and, in fact, ask why we should imagine God as having only one essential gender rather than two? Mary Daley, for example, implores us to use "bisexual imagery" for the "Father-Mother God,"[5] and there have been, of course, some religious traditions that portray their deities as bi-gendered, such as the Aztec Ometeotl and the Norse Loki. Even in *DC vs. Marvel*, a graphic novel not officially part of either the DC or Marvel universes, we read, "In the beginning there were two entities... 'brothers' although they were also sisters, sexless and everything in between."

In response to this, I'd say that in the case of God, Ometeotl, Loki, "the brothers" or whoever, the proposition "A deity can have more than one gender" is likely false on account of its probable incoherence. Without getting ahead of myself, if I were to define the masculine in terms of taking care of, providing for, and protecting the feminine, and the feminine as being receptive to these masculine gestures, then what would it mean for God to do this to Himself? For God to love Himself is one thing, given that we all understand what it

---

3    John Cooper, *Our Father in Heaven: Christian Faith and Inclusive Language for God* (Grand Rapids, MI: Baker Books, 1998), 284.
4    C. S. Lewis, *Perelandra*, in *The Cosmic Trilogy* by C. S. Lewis (London: Pan Books, 1990), 327-328.
5    Mary Daly, "After the Death of God the Father: Women's Liberation and the Transformation of Christian Consciousness," in *Woman Spirit Rising: A Feminist Reader in Religion*, ed. Carol Christ and Judith Plaskow (San Francisco: HarperSanFrancisco, 1992), 59.

means to love ourselves. But for God to demonstrate the dance of the genders within Himself and toward Himself seems implausible. I cannot imagine what this would look like and we certainly have no biblical evidence for this. Even in Trinitarian theology, the Father, Son, and Spirit are, individually and most consistently, spoken of in masculine terms, strongly suggesting that masculinity, like omniscience, omnipotence, and love is something shared by the God-head substance, and not something belonging solely to the personality properties of each Divine Person.

Nonetheless, some will further object: if God made females, He must be the originator of this idea, and does this not suggest He is, if we must attribute gender to God at all, equally feminine? Not at all. To be sure, God is the originator of females and the feminine, but He is probably so not by "being" but by "possessing the idea of." In other words, while He would have the essential property "being masculine," He would have the essential property "possessing the idea of femininity." To clarify, we might say that while God has the essential properties of "possessing the idea of wings," "possessing the idea of rain," or even "possessing the idea of murder," He is neither a winged being nor rain nor a murderer. Thus, on this model—which is in keeping with the orthodox Christian, DC and Marvel models—God is God, and not goddess, but He, of course, made all things that are feminine from His eternal idea of femininity, which, I hasten to add, is a very beautiful idea indeed.

When it comes to created gendered beings, superhero mythology does occasionally diverge a bit from the model I present. For example, in the DC universe, we know Martian Manhunter is "technically asexual,"[6] and in the Marvel universe, the Norse god Loki is bi-gendered. But if God—the Spirit, Rational Soul, Person or Original Substance—is essentially masculine and it is, as I argue, incoherent for Him also to be essentially feminine, then it seems probable that those created in His image[7]—other spirits, persons or rational souls—would also be essentially gendered (I leave non-rational souls, such as animals, to the side). Consequently, insofar as Martian Manhunter and Loki can be understood to be created rational beings, a more coherent depiction of them would have been to depict them as essentially of one gender or another, but not genderless nor bi-gendered.

Certainly this seems to be the most in keeping with the Bible and even the general contours of polytheism. In the case of the Bible, it does not explicitly say that angelic beings—polytheism's gods and goddesses if we like—are made in God's image, yet we can infer this through other essential properties

---

6   *JLA: Golden Perfect.*
7   In DC's *Day of Judgment*, the biblical notion that human beings are created in God's "image" is affirmed. Of course, DC says nothing about other types of created rational souls like martians.

they possess which seem to belong exclusively to spirits or rational souls. Among other things, angels have the ultimate capacity for free will (hence, St. Paul refers to the "elect angels"[8]), and they have the ultimate capacity for rationality (hence, Satan, Gabriel and others challenge, calculate, argue, tempt, deliver messages, etc.). But do we have biblical evidence for created spirits—specifically, angels—being gendered? I think we do.

In addition to the (admittedly weak) testimony of some Bible-believing Christians who underwent near-death experiences and actually saw gendered angels,[9] the Bible consistently speaks of the major angels or demons in masculine terms. Some have objected to this, however, saying that because there is no Hebrew neuter term, the masculine was used instead. But this is unconvincing for many reasons, none more than the fact that even though in Greek there is a neuter term, none of the proper names of angels are in the neuter.[10]

That angels are depicted as gendered is fairly clear. But are all angels *masculine*? Are there only "gods" and no "goddesses"? The Hebrew and Greek words for the general class "angel" always refer to them in the masculine, but this, in itself, is philosophically uninteresting. Human beings, when referred to collectively, have traditionally been classified in the masculine ("man"). Insofar as masculinity contains within itself the notions of representation or authority, it is quite proper to use the masculine to cover both the masculine and feminine. Moreover, even if the Bible did not mention any feminine angels, it would hardly follow that none exist. Nevertheless, I do think we have some concrete evidence for feminine angels, not only, again, from the testimony of people with near death experiences, but also in the Bible itself. In Zechariah 5:9, we read, "Then I looked up—and there before me were two women with the wind in their wings!" Almost certainly this verse doesn't refer to human women since humans don't have wings. However, angels appear to possess them. Because it is not very clear what these winged women would be metaphors of, it seems possible that this verse is depicting actual feminine angels. But, even if this reading is wrong, it seems very probable that angels, as with God, are gendered spirits, and so we can say with relative confidence that whatever else Jesus means when He says we will "be like the angels" in

---

8   1 Timothy 5:21.
9   Gary Habermas and J. P. Moreland, *Beyond Death: Exploring the Evidence for Immortality* (Eugene, OR: Wipf & Stock, 1998), 157.
10   This is just one example of many, but in Matthew 25:41 we read, "*hetoimasmenon to Diabolo kai tois angelois autou*" ("having prepared for the Devil and *his* angels"). The word "Devil" (*Diabolo*) is masculine in the Greek and so is the possessive pronoun "his" (*autou*). The chauvinistic attitudes of some in the Middle Ages prompted a few, like Michelangelo, to depict the Devil as feminine.

Heaven, He is not denying us our essential gender.[11]

So, from the Uncreated Spirit (God) and the created angelic spirits (angels, "gods" and even, perhaps, martians), we finally arrive at created human spirits. Orthodoxy has usually maintained that the biblical understanding of a human being is that of a spirit, person, or rational soul which has the ultimate capacity to develop and possess a body.[12] We *are* souls and we *have* (most of the time) bodies. Of course, the connection between the soul and body is extremely tight, but for my purposes here, their distinction needs to be noted.

If God and angels—the two other spirit types that we know of—are essentially gendered, then it seems likely that humans would be as well. This argument can be further strengthened not only by some out-of-body experiences wherein the disembodied person recognizes himself or herself and other family members by their gendered qualities,[13] but also by biblical evidence, where those who appeared after death, such as Samuel, Elijah, Moses, and Jesus, were recognizably gendered.[14] Moreover, since human bodies are distinguished by their sex (I leave difficult cases of sexual ambiguity to the side for the moment), it seems that human spirits are sandwiched between God and angels—gendered spirits—from above and sexed bodies from below. Very likely, then, we should think of ourselves, in our inner self, spirit, or soul, as being essentially gendered, either masculine or feminine,[15] and, for the most part, this is generally how the DC and Marvel universes depict human beings as well.

The rightness of this, moreover, does seem supported by a lot of work done in anthropology and psychology. Andrew Tolson, for example, thinks a "deep structure of masculinity"[16] can be observed. Thomas Gregor insists, after his study in the Amazon, that "there are continuities of masculinity that transcend cultural differences."[17] Walter Lonner believes culture "is only a thin veneer covering an essential universal" gender dimorphism.[18] John Williams

---

11  Cf. John Frame, "Men and Women in the Image of God," in *Recovering Biblical Manhood and Woman*, ed. John Piper and Wayne Grudem (Wheaton, IL: Crossway, 1991), 232.
12  For a defense of this claim, see J. P. Moreland and Scott Rae, *Body & Soul: Human Nature & the Crisis in Ethics* (Downers Grove, IL: IVP, 2000), 17-47.
13  Habermas and Moreland, *Beyond Death*, 162.
14  1 Samuel 28:11-15, Matthew 17:1-13, John 20:25-27, and Revelation 11:1-12.
15  See C. S. Lewis, *Miracles* (New York: Macmillan, 1947), 165-166. Cf. John Gilmore, *Probing Heaven* (Grand Rapids, MI: Baker, 1989), 80-90.
16  Andrew Tolson, *The Limits of Masculinity: Male Identity and the Liberated Woman* (New York: Harper and Row, 1977), 56.
17  Thomas Gregor, *Anxious Pleasures: The Sexual Life of an Amazonian People* (Chicago: University of Chicago Press, 1985), 209.
18  Walter Lonner, "The Search for Psychological Universals," in *Handbook of Cross-*

and Deborah Best, in their study of thirty different cultures, say there is "substantial similarity" to be found "panculturally in the traits ascribed to men and women."[19] And David Gilmore, not at all dismissive of cultural anomalies, concludes: "[T]here is a recurring notion in world cultures that real manhood is different from simple anatomical maleness."[20]

Nonetheless, gender is one thing, sex is another. In both the DC and Marvel universes we see examples of souls who are moved, regenerated or reincarnated into different bodies. In *DC Universe Presents* vol. 1, Boston Brand, a masculine spirit, is shown to have once been incarnate as a woman, and, indeed, a stripper.[21] And in Marvel's *X-Men: Original Sin*, Mr. Sinister creates for himself a new body, which is now female. When Professor X realizes this and says, "You're Sinister, Dear God!" Sinister replies, "Well, kind of, minus the Y chromosome, of course. But who needs that old thing?" In both these cases, the implication is that the gender of the soul doesn't strongly relate to the sex of the body, and this, I suggest, is a mistake.

Because a general principle in both the Bible and Nature seems to be that the higher guides, controls, or otherwise affects the lower, the human spirit (which is higher) would guide, control, or affect the physical body (which is lower). I read Thomas Aquinas's formulation of the soul-body interaction to be more or less the correct one here.[22]

In terms of gender and sex, what this means is that if your soul has the essential property "being masculine," then your soul, which guides the development of your body, would see to it that your body develops the corresponding sex, which is male. You are masculine and your body will likely reflect this insofar as you have male parts. Or again, if your soul has the essential property of being feminine, then your body will likely have

---

*Cultural Psychology*, ed. Harry Triandis and William Lambert (Boston: Allyn and Bacon, 1980), 1437.
19 John Williams and Deborah Best, *Measuring Sex Stereotypes: A Thirty-Nation Study* (Beverly Hills, CA: Sage, 1982), 30.
20 David Gilmore, *Manhood in the Making: Cultural Concepts of Masculinity* (New Haven: Yale University Press, 1990), 11.
21 Additionally, in *Batman: The Brave and the Bold*, black magic causes Batman's masculine soul to be placed in Bat Lady's female body, and Bat Lady's feminine soul to be placed in Batman's male body. *Batman: The Brave and the Bold* season 2, episode 21.
22 Thomas Aquinas *Summa Theologica* Ia, Q. 76, art. 6-8. This is not to deny that the lower can also affect the higher. The experience we gain through the body and brain does enter into the mind and soul and becomes a permanent part of the soul. Nevertheless, based on the greater-over-the-lesser principle, the soul probably does affect and guide the development of the body in a greater and more substantial way than the body does the soul.

female biology. You, then, would be feminine, and your body would be female. General biological differences, including general brain differences, then, are determined by the soul, though, of course, the Fall may have caused some disconnect here as we'll see when we talk about disabilities.

Whatever the case, the generalities of this model fit fairly well with the latest research in biology. Physicians Gaya Arnaoff and Jennifer Bell of Columbia University posited recently, "There is increasing evidence to suggest that the brain is a sexual organ, that brain sex (i.e., the sex of the brain) is paramount in determining human gender identity."[23] Though I think they have it backwards—that gender determines sex rather than sex, gender—we may take their claim to be evidence that sexual biology is far from fluid. Even at birth, the sexual differences are present and significant, pace what some have imagined. As Leonard Sax succinctly explains:

> In men, many areas of the brain are rich in proteins that are coded directly by the Y chromosome. Those proteins are absent in women's brain tissue. Conversely, women's brain tissue is rich in material coded directly by the X chromosome; these particular transcripts of the X chromosome are absent from men's brain tissue. These sex differences, then, are *genetically programmed*, not mediated by hormonal differences. . . . They are present at birth.[24]

These programmed sex differences do result in many different concrete ways that boys and girls play and learn, even though, and this hardly needs to be said, *differences do not imply any kind of absolute superiority*. Quoting Sax again, "The bottom line is that the brain is just organized *differently* in females and males. The tired argument about which sex is more intelligent or which sex has the 'better' brain is about as meaningful as arguing about which utensil is 'better,' a knife or a spoon. The only correct answer to such a question is: 'Better for what?'"[25]

Insofar as non-human rational souls can take on physical bodies, the pattern of gendered souls programming sexed bodies is likely true here as well.[26] Thus, in Genesis 6:1-8, the "sons of God"—which the Old Testament

---

23 Gaya Aranoff and Jennifer Bell, "Endocrinology and Growth in Children and Adolescents," in *Principles of Gender-Specific Medicine*, ed. Marianne Legato (New York: Academic Press, 2004), 12.
24 Leonard Sax, *Why Gender Matters* (New York: Broadway, 2005), 14-15. See Arthur Arnold and Paul Burgoyne, "Are XX and XY Brain Cells Intrinsically Different?" *Trends in Endocrinology and Metabolism* 15 (2004): 6-11.
25 Sax, *Why Gender Matters*, 32.
26 I do not have room here to address the complexities of the animal kingdom, though typically Christianity agrees with many polytheistic and shamanistic systems in maintaining that animals have souls, albeit non-rational, mortal souls. If this is the

always refers to as angels[27]—appear to have taken on a biological form and had sex with "the daughters of men," producing the *nephilim* or giants. This, perhaps, is the historical basis for polytheism's stories about the philandering gods—stories that are repeated and developed in superhero mythology. Even in the case of Spirit Himself, we can infer that if God is masculine, then it makes perfect sense that His incarnate body would be male. In other words, it is probably not at all accidental that Jesus was born a man and not a woman.

## THE DUTIES OF GENDER

As I mentioned earlier, one of the glories of superhero mythology is that there are both masculine and feminine superheroes. And although these aren't always depicted as essentially gendered, most of the time they are, which, as I have argued, is as it should be.[28] Yet how should the masculine and feminine act? What moral duties, if any, come with gendered properties? And more specifically, how should gendered superheroes act? Let's first take a look at how gender duties were originally portrayed in superhero mythology before moving on to definitions and philosophical critique.

In *The Supergirls: Fashion, Feminism, Fantasy and the History of Comic Book Heroines*, Mike Madrid argues that the first superheroines "were given powers that are weaker than their male compatriots, and positions of lesser importance."[29] While masculine superheroes were typically given names with the word "man" in it (Super*man*, Bat*man*, Spider-*Man*, etc.), the feminine superheroes were typically given names with the word "girl" in it (Bat*girl*, Super*girl*, Marvel *Girl*, Invisible *Girl*, etc.). Some masculine heroes, such as Captain Marvel, even named their feminine counterparts, such as Mary Marvel, in much the same way that the biblical Adam, who was given a

---

case, then it seems possible that their souls or substances would contain the blueprints for determining the sex of their bodies as well, though it's certainly possible that some of these creatures, not made in the image of God, would lack a gender property and thus could, consistent with my model, be asexual, for example.

27 "Now there was a day when *the sons of God* came to present themselves before the Lord, Satan also came among them" (Job 1:6); "Again there was a day when *the sons of God* came to present themselves before the Lord, and Satan came among them to present himself before the Lord" (Job 2:1); and "Where were you when the morning stars sang together, and all *the sons of God* shouted for joy?" (Job 38:7). Emphasis added.

28 Martian Manhunter and Loki problematize gender essentialism in the DC and Marvel universes; nevertheless, they are the exceptions. More typical is the essentialism of someone like Wonder Woman, who rightly speaks of "the gender [people] were born to." *Wonder Woman: The Greatest Stories Ever Told*.

29 Mike Madrid, *The Supergirls: Fashion, Feminism, Fantasy and the History of Comic Book Heroines* (n.p.: Exterminating Angel Press, 2010), vi.

limited authority over Eve, names her. The overall effect of this is that the early feminine superheroes of the '30s, '40s and '50s were generally expected to help or assist masculine superheroes, just as women during World War II were expected to help men fight the war by making ammunition and supplies in factories. This is to say that both men and women were expected to be brave, hardworking and so on, but they were expected to do so in keeping with, and not against, their gendered natures—where women were expected, among other things, to assist men, and men were expected, among other things, to lead women. The "feminism" of early superhero mythology, in other words, extends to saying that people are equal as people—equal as persons with the call to demonstrate their ultimate capacities for virtue, rationality and so on—but not equal as masculine or feminine beings (the two being, not better or worse, but certainly different). Thus, even into the '70s, the reductive feminism that denies gender uniqueness was largely associated with evil and perversion in many superhero stories; for example, in "Come on in . . . the Revolution's Fine!" the wicked Enchantress tries to divide the Avengers by convincing the Wasp, Black Widow and other feminine superheroes to reject the supportive roles that they had traditionally played; yet in the end, the Enchantress was exposed and Goliath, admittedly not the most tactful of the masculine superheroes, says, "I hope you birds finally learned your lesson about that woman's lib bull!"[30]

Wonder Woman, however, was a bit of an exception. Wonder Woman was created by William Moulton Marston, an eccentric psychologist and social philosopher. Marston strongly advocated matriarchy because he believed that if women were in charge, the world would be a more peaceful place. Moreover, he believed that the only way women could ever be put in charge was if they used their sexuality to dominate men, making males the happy servants of females. Marston created Wonder Woman—an Amazon or a woman free of patriarchal rule—to popularize his social agenda; he writes,

> Frankly, Wonder Woman is psychological propaganda for the new type of woman who should, I believe, rule the world. There isn't love enough in the male organism to run this planet peacefully. Woman's body contains twice as many love generating organs and endocrine mechanisms as the male. What woman lacks is the dominance or self-assertive power to put over and enforce her love desires. I have given Wonder Woman this dominant force but have kept her loving, tender, maternal and feminine in every other way. Her bracelets . . . represent . . . submission to Aphrodite, Goddess of Love and Beauty. Her magic lasso, which compels anyone bound by it to obey Wonder Woman and which was given to her by Aphrodite herself, represents woman's love

---

30  Ibid., 150.

charm and allure by which she compels men and women to do her bidding.[31]

The irony of this, however, is that in nearly every early issue of *Wonder Woman*, we see scantily clad women—often Wonder Woman herself—in bondage, suggesting not the sexual strength but weakness of women. Indeed, Marston himself seems to have been a bit of a hypocrite here since he lived very much a patriarchal life in a polygamous relationship with two women.[32]

Despite the oddities surrounding Wonder Woman's origin and early stories, she is generally considered the "first feminist in pop fiction"[33] and was even an inspiration to feminist champion Gloria Steinem[34] because the Princess of Power didn't see her heroics as simply supporting masculine ones. Nevertheless, Marston's original matriarchal agenda for Wonder Woman disappeared over the years[35] to the point where she is now seen, in the words of Lois Lane,[36] as a "God's-Honest-Post-Feminist Woman with a capital W" because Wonder Woman "only" demands that the sexes (and genders) be treated equal in all respects.[37] Thus, when her mother, Queen Hippolyta, invades Washington DC, hoping to enslave the men of the world, Wonder Woman opposes her "on the side of Justice."[38]

So which of these three views of gender and superheroes is most in keeping with an orthodox Christian understanding of the duties of the genders? Are men and woman equal as persons but different in gender duties, with the feminine supporting masculine leadership (as with most of the early superheroes)? Are men and women equal as persons but different in gender duties, with the masculine supporting feminine leadership (as with Marston)?

---

31  Les Daniels, *Wonder Woman: The Complete History* (San Francisco: Chronicle Books, 2004), 22-23.
32  Ibid., 28.
33  Ibid., 201.
34  Marc DiPaolo, *War, Politics and Superheroes: Ethics and Propaganda in Comics and Film* (Jefferson, NC: McFarland, 2011), 24.
35  Of course, this is for the most part. Some writers, especially in the '50s, depicted Wonder Woman very much like the other supportive heroines, and this partly had to do with the 1950s Comics Code, which, in an attempt to reduce overly-sexual portrayals of women, states, "The inclusion of females in stories is specifically discouraged. Women, when used in a plot structure, should be secondary in importance." In Madrid, *The Supergirls*, 77.
36  Although Lois Lane is often thought of as a feminist, she herself happily admits, "I tried to be the strong independent woman with something to say, and I ended up making my career by standing behind a man [Superman]. I'm a bad feminist." *Superman: Grounded* vol. 1.
37  *Wonder Woman: The Greatest Stories Every Told.*
38  *Wonder Woman: Amazons Attack!*

Or are men and women equal as persons and equal in gender duties of support and leadership (as with the later Wonder Woman)?

John Piper gives a decent orthodox Christian definition of the genders, seeing masculinity as "a sense of benevolent responsibility to lead, provide for and protect women in ways appropriate to a man's differing relationships," and femininity as "a freeing disposition to affirm, receive and nurture strength and leadership from worthy men in ways appropriate to a woman's differing relationships."[39] In keeping with gender being a property of the soul, I'd modify this slightly; so instead of saying that masculinity has within it the disposition "to protect women," we should rather say that it has within itself the disposition "to protect the feminine," and instead of saying that femininity seeks to strengthen "worthy men," we should say that it seeks to strengthen "the worthy masculine." In this way these definitions can properly apply to all rational souls, including God, angels, and humans.[40] Moreover, we must be clear that the dispositions Piper mentions come with general moral obligations. Masculine souls should generally act in keeping with their masculine property, and feminine souls should generally act in keeping with their feminine one. In the case of God, for example, we should expect to see Him act in keeping with His masculine nature, and, according to Robert Conant, this is exactly what we do in fact see (leading him to say of Christ, for instance, "He was the supremely manly man"[41]). Finally, because when a person acts in keeping with

---

39  John Piper, "A Vision of Biblical Complementarity," in *Recovering Biblical Manhood and Woman*, ed. John Piper and Wayne Grudem (Wheaton, IL: Crossway, 1991), 35-36. Leonard Sax says consistently, but more vaguely, "being a man means using your strength in the service of others." Leonard Sax, *Boys Adrift* (New York: Basic Books, 2007), 181.

40  God is the Eternal Masculine and so defines Himself partly through His eternal idea of the feminine. This literal truth is often expressed metaphorically when we talk about God's relation to Israel or the Church. God the masculine protects the creation, which, metaphorically, is feminine in relation to Him (His "wife" or "bride"), but these, as I said earlier, are metaphors. God is essentially and literally masculine, but He is not literally a husband or bridegroom since the Christian idea of marriage is between one man (masculine) and one woman (feminine), and this would not at all work if God, the Prime Masculine, were to be cast as married to billions of Christian men! Thus, God is essentially and literally masculine; the creation is metaphorically feminine in relation to him. To speak personally, I am essentially and literally masculine and my wife is essentially and literally feminine, but we are metaphorically feminine in relation to God. These metaphors are valuable and do agree with my revised Piper definition of masculinity and femininity: that the masculine has a sense of benevolent authority over, and responsibility to protect, that which is feminine, while the feminine has the sense of submission and the responsibility to strengthen, support and ennoble that which is masculine.

41  Robert Conant, *The Virility of Christ* (Chicago: n. p., 1915), 117.

his or her essential properties or nature, the person can be said to act justly, and because the person who acts justly is the person who pleases God, and because God's pleasure secures our happiness (God knows what will make us ultimately happy), we can say that the man who acts in keeping with his masculine nature—the man of masculine virtue or the "manly" man—and the woman who acts in keeping with her feminine nature—the woman of feminine virtue or the "womanly" woman—will flourish in these capacities.

Given all this, it should be clear that the early depiction of gender and superheroes—of feminine superheroes supporting the masculine ones and the masculine ones leading well—is the depiction most in keeping with orthodox Christianity and my revised Piper definition. Nevertheless, I want to go a bit beyond these generalities and test the orthodox understanding against a number of concrete scenarios in superhero mythology. And as is proper, I'll start with ladies first.

The early feminine superheroes were brave, hardworking and skilled in battle, yet they recognized that these goods must be in keeping with their feminine nature, which is to say they should support, strengthen and submit to worthy masculine leadership. Supergirl supports Superman, Batgirl supports Batman, and Mary Marvel supports Captain Marvel. These girls demonstrate both the virtue of bravery and the virtue of womanliness in their superheroics, and, far from being restricted in their potential as Madrid argues, they actually flourish in more capacities than Wonder Woman does, for example, since they, unlike her, are not only brave—which is proper to all persons[42]—but they are also womanly—which is proper to feminine souls.[43] In this way, Fredric Wertham is partially right and partially wrong when he says of Wonder Woman, "She is an undesirable ideal for girls, being the exact opposite of what girls are supposed to want to be."[44]

Yet speaking now specifically about Wonder Woman, should we say that she somehow ceases to be a feminine soul when she doesn't act womanly? No;

---

42  Just as both the genders can be courageous so too can both the genders be physically strong. Courage and strength aren't "masculine" per se. A woman isn't less a woman if she is physically strong, just as a man isn't less a man if he is physically weak. In this way, when Peter Parker's basketball coach calls Peter "a woman" for shooting the ball badly (*Ultimate Spider-Man Omnibus* vol. 1), or the Hulk says Korg "hits like a girl" because he doesn't hit as hard as himself (*The Incredible Hulk* vol. 1, #620 [January 2011]), we should see these insults as unjust, or at least, unhelpful. Certainly on the whole men are physically stronger than women, but physical strength isn't exclusively a man's thing. True, men might need physical strength more than women in order to achieve their goals, one of which is to protect the feminine, but even so, there is nothing wrong with a woman being physically strong per se.
43  Madrid, *The Supergirls*, vi.
44  Ibid., 190.

this would be to confuse metaphysics and ethics, to confuse *being something* and *flourishing in being that something*. Consider two examples.

In the 2009 animated movie *Wonder Woman*, Wonder Woman is initially a bit offended by Steve Trevor's masculine gesture of opening the door for her; she says, "I lift cars; I can lift car door handles." Here it's true that Wonder Woman, as a physically strong person, can open her own doors, and, in fact, is physically strengthened by doing so; nevertheless, by opening her own doors—or, more to the point, by refusing an appropriate masculine gesture of provision—she fails to flourish in her feminine capacity, which, as a spiritual capacity, is far more important than a mere physical one. Wonder Woman remains a feminine soul, yet doesn't strengthen herself in this way because of her insistence that gender is unimportant. By doing everything for herself, she is less strong than if she let a man do something for her on appropriate occasions.

Or again, consider Wonder Woman's costume.[45] Of all the early superheroines, Wonder Woman's is the skimpiest; in *Sensation Comics* vol. 1, #2, she even says, "Lucky this outfit was in my bag. I can do better with fewer clothes!" While I suppose this might be a practical consideration in battle (!) and while it certainly highlights her admittedly beautiful female form, Wonder Woman's felt need to wear fewer clothes is a stumbling block to her own feminine flourishing. That is, because the feminine is supposed to nurture strength, and not weakness, in the masculine, females who dress skimpily outside of proper contexts (such as in the marriage bed) can rightly be said, in their immodesty, to hinder masculine flourishing. Men, of course, can't use the appearance of a woman as an excuse for their own unjust behavior (lust); nevertheless, an immodestly dressed woman certainly will hinder even the most temperate men from acting manly toward them. Thus, once again, the sexy feminist Wonder Woman, while certainly a feminine soul, doesn't flourish much in respect to her femininity.

But what about masculine superheroes? Let's consider two examples of how masculine superheroes flourish, or fail to flourish, in respect to their gender. The first example has to do with physical violence against women, and the second has to do with fornication.

---

45  I don't have room to discuss it fully, but cross-dressing, which is generally forbidden in the Bible (see Deuteronomy 22:5), is another instance of an attempt to subvert gender roles. For a woman to dress as a man—unless there is a very good reason to do so—is for a woman not to act as a woman, and for a man to dress as a woman is for a man not to act as a man. Cultures may reasonably differ to some extent on the kinds of things they consider cross-dressing or gender-bending (Are jeans on women cross-dressing? Are shaved legs on men?); nevertheless, the obligation for each gender to act according to its nature remains fundamental.

In the case of physical violence against women, we have examples of both a hero like Ant-Man, and a villain like the Joker, abusing women: Ant-Man slaps his girlfriend/wife, the Wasp,[46] and the Joker shoots Batgirl.[47] In both cases, Ant-Man and the Joker, as masculine beings, are generally called to protect women, not abuse them, and insofar as the violence against these women is excessive, these men fail to act manly. They are men, but not manly men. Indeed, they stand in stark contrast with countless superheroes (and even the occasional super-villain[48]) who are well-aware of the general masculine prohibition against hitting women: in *Superhero Squad*, the Hulk says, "Hulk no hit girls" (and so shouts at them rather);[49] in *The Avengers: Kree/Skrull War*, Captain Mar-vel says, "One prejudice ingrained in me during my time on Earth . . . is that I never strike a lady;" in *Captain America Lives! Omnibus*, Isaiah Bradley, the black Captain America, says, "I don't like hittin' girls;" in *Avengers vs. X-Men*, Thor tells Emma Frost, "I have no wish to lay hands on a maiden;" in *Green Lantern/Green Arrow*, Green Arrow thinks to himself, "I can't bring myself to strike a woman;" and in one of the earliest issues of *The X-Men*, Stan Lee told Roy Thomas, the author of the series, to change the villain Banshee from a female to a male because it looked very unheroic for a group of superheroes to be fighting a lone woman.[50] Of course, striking a woman is a *general* moral prohibition like "Don't kill," "Don't deceive" or "Don't work on the Sabbath," and not an *absolute* one like "Don't murder," "Don't lie" or "Don't blaspheme God;" thus, there are times when striking a woman might be the *right* or *just* thing to do, and in this, Batman is correct when he says, "The hammer of justice is unisex."[51] Nevertheless, even in these moments of just necessity, the manly man should feel bad that this was necessary; he should lament that what is just isn't always the same as what is ideal; hence, in *Secret War*, Captain America tells Nick Fury, "I bashed the girl [super-villain] in the face with the other one's flying glider. Not my proudest moment." Here masculine superheroes are more heroic because they act in keeping with, and not against or disregarding, their gender.

In the case of fornication—in particular, sex before marriage—we have some cases of masculine superheroes whose heroics are diminished by engaging in this practice. Why would this diminish their masculinity? In the Bible, but also probably in Nature, it's fairly clear that sex outside of marriage

---

46  *The Ultimates: Super-Human*.
47  *Batman: The Killing Joke*.
48  In *Fantastic Four: The Trial of Galactus*, Invisible Woman realizes she's fighting a Doom-bot and not Dr. Doom himself because Dr. Doom, despite being a super-villain, wouldn't "strike a woman."
49  *Superhero Squad* season 1, episode 24.
50  *Marvel Chronicle: A Year by Year History* (New York: DK, 2008), 120.
51  *Batman: The Brave and the Bold* season 1, episode 15.

## Christian Philosophy and Superhero Mythology

is unjust.[52] To engage in this, moreover, is not simply for individuals to be unjust to God, who has told us how sex should and shouldn't be done, but it is also to be unjust or spiritually harmful to each other.[53] In particular, men are supposed to protect women and insofar as a man pursues, asks for or even simply accepts sex from a woman outside of marriage, this man, while still being a masculine spirit, does not flourish in his masculinity since he does not act manly. This is one of the major problems with many modern retellings of superhero myths. In the past, partly due to the Comics Code[54] but also partly due to a clearer understanding of the injustice of fornication, no superhero had sex before marriage, and many superheroes, such as Mister Fantastic and Spider-Man, valued marriage deeply. Indeed, even the villains didn't rape, but rather attempted to trick girls into marrying them![55] But nowadays, DC and Marvel have largely and foolishly accepted that sex before marriage is just, and so have not seen a conflict in showing their heroes, even their marquee heroes, engaging in this practice. Superman,[56] Batman,[57] Captain America,[58] Colossus,[59] Cyclops,[60] Daredevil,[61] and others have all, at one time or another, had sex before marriage. In this way, DC and Marvel have actually made their heroes, even their greatest heroes, a little less heroic because they have made them a little less moral. These heroes are masculine, but they aren't, at least

---

52  1 Corinthians 7:2. The high value of marriage in ancient cultures across the world strongly suggests that people have some general sense that sex outside of marriage, including before marriage, is bad.

53  She-Hulk, the feminine, is certainly right when she points out the double-standard between fornicating men and fornicating women; as she says to Iron Man, "When you do it, everyone calls you a player. When I do it, they call me a skank." Madrid, *The Supergirls*, 260. Certainly, this is a double-standard, and so I think both fornicating men and fornicating women should be called "skanks" or something of that sort.

54  "The treatment of love-romance stories shall emphasize the home and the sanctity of marriage." Amy Kiste Nyberg, *Seal of Approval: The History of the Comics Code* (Jackson, MISS: University Press of Mississippi, 1998), 168.

55  Thus, in *Journey into Mystery* vol. 1, #83 (August 1962), the Executioner (a villain, but not the Asgardian super-villain) demands that Jane Foster marry him if she doesn't want to see Donald Blake (Thor) killed; he says, "You like him, eh? Tell me what you would do to save his life? Would you marry me?"

56  In *Smallville* Clark has sex with both Lana and Lois even though he was married to neither.

57  *Batman Incorporated*.

58  Captain America isn't married to Sharon Carter, but she becomes pregnant with his child in *Captain America: The Death of Captain America*.

59  *Astonishing X-Men: Ultimate Collection* vol. 2.

60  Ibid.

61  *Daredevil: Guardian Devil*.

in these limited moments, manly. Physically harming a woman is generally unmanly, but so is having consensual sex with her outside of marriage. Neither way is how masculine spirits, and especially masculine superheroes, should behave.

ABOVE: ON THE LEFT, THE DEVILISH MEPHISTO SHOWS HIMSELF TO BE THE ENEMY OF GOD AND MARRIAGE WHEN HE TEMPTS PETER PARKER IN *THE AMAZING SPIDER-MAN: ONE MORE DAY*; AND ON THE RIGHT, SUPERMAN ACTS NOT ONLY SACRIFICIALLY, WHICH IS PROPER TO ALL HEROES, BUT ALSO MANLY, WHICH IS PROPER TO MASCULINE ONES, BY PROTECTING NOT JUST BARE PERSONS BUT FEMININE PERSONS LIKE WONDER WOMAN IN *TRINITY*.

Consequently, while I think it desirable to have both masculine and feminine superheroes, neither type of superhero should ignore their gender duties in the course of their heroics, for to do so is to diminish their heroics. To be sure, gender considerations certainly complicate heroics, but this is inevitable if one's heroics are to be true heroics since gender duties are moral duties and moral duties are the foundation of heroics. And although it's rarely easy to decide what the heroic course of action is, wisdom would have us consider all the relevant factors and moral duties and then implement them with conviction.

Thus, to give one final example, if we were to imagine Batgirl and Robin as bare humans, stripped of their particularities of gender, age and so on, and if they fell into danger, then Batman, stripped of all his particularities, should try to save both equally. But none of these three are bare humans; they are, among other things, gendered humans, and gender matters in our moral reasoning. Thus, Batman (the masculine) has a duty to Batgirl (the feminine) which he doesn't have to Robin (the masculine).[62] Or again, suppose

---

62  True, Batman (the father) has a duty to Robin (the son) that he doesn't have to Batgirl (an acquaintance), but that's another matter. For more on fathers and sons, and the duties of fathers to sons, see *Batman and Robin: Born to Kill*.

Batman were in danger this time and it was up to Batgirl or Robin to save him. Here it would be preferable to have Robin save Batman since the masculine rescuing the masculine is less problematic than the feminine rescuing the masculine. But let's imagine that Robin is out of the picture, and it's up to Batgirl or nobody. This situation isn't ideal insofar as womanliness has to do with receiving protection from the masculine rather than offering it to the masculine; nevertheless, since it's far better that Batgirl show courage and love by saving Batman than by doing nothing in the name of womanliness, Batgirl ought to save him. We live in a non-ideal world, and we must do the best we can. Female heroics have their place and we can celebrate them therein. Yet even so, we should always long to see the genders act optimally or ideally in all that they do. Thus, although Green Lantern is wrong to refuse Wonder Woman's rescue in *Justice League: Origin*, we should certainly understand why he "hates being rescued by her." And although Wonder Woman is "The most powerful woman on the planet," we should certainly delight in the fact that both weak men like Steve Trevor[63] and strong men like Superman, "INSIST on protecting her."[64]

## DISABILITY AND SEXUAL ORIENTATION

Orthodox Christians generally accept that there is a historical basis for the mythical framework of creation, fall and redemption. In particular, orthodox Christians accept that because Adam was given authority over the Earth, all those below him had the potential to be either blessed by his good choices or cursed by his bad ones. And because Adam made bad choices, choosing to love a lesser (his wife) over the greater (God), he became unrighteous and subsequently brought God's just curse ("the lesser shall rebel against the greater") upon himself and all those under his authority. Moreover, the effects of this "lesser-against-the-greater" curse can properly be called disabling or disability-producing, where a disability can roughly be defined as a physical or spiritual impairment that limits one or more of the major life activities of an individual.[65]

Physically speaking, the two key disabilities that all humans suffer from are poor physical healing and bodily death, both of which can be seen

---

63 *Wonder Woman: The Greatest Stories Every Told.*
64 In *Trinity*, Wonder Woman is shocked by her own feminine response to Superman, the masculine, saving her; on repeated pages, she says, "Again, he moves to protect me. Such a ... man. ... Again, he moves to protect me."
65 Here I have modified the definition of a disability given by the Americans with Disabilities Act, which talks about "mental impairment" rather than the broader "spiritual impairment." "Americans with Disabilities Act (1990)," *U. S. Statutes at Large*, vol. 104, 327-378.

as the lesser (the body) "rebelling" against the greater (the soul). Before the human Fall, I think it likely that when Adam and Eve were inflicted with pain (from falling from a mountain, stepping on a twig, or whatever), their bodies, designed to be immortal, would have healed much the way Wolverine's does. Because they had the potential to feel pleasure, they probably also had the potential to feel pain, yet the pain they would have felt probably would have been brief, and certainly wouldn't have killed them. However, after the Fall, human bodies don't heal nearly as well, and while all suffer from this in general, those who are blinded in this life and cannot regain their sight, such as Daredevil, or those who are made lame in this life and cannot regain the proper use of their legs, such as Professor X or Oracle, suffer from the disability of poor bodily healing more acutely than others, which is why they are sometimes called "disabled" proper.

Spiritually speaking, the Fall disables humanity in many ways as well. Most relevant to our discussion of gender is the disability that causes our emotions or desires to rebel against our reason (again, "the lesser against the greater"), and the disability that comes from the soul misprogramming the body via its DNA.[66] Since both of these aspects are connected with homosexual orientation, I'll deal with them together and work these out in and through some superhero myths.

From the beginning, *X-Men* stories have been wonderful vehicles to discuss the rights of minorities and the marginalized. The X-Men aren't normal human beings; they are mutants; their souls, using my language, have programmed their DNA with genetic anomalies. Sometimes these anomalies are seen as a "disease"[67] or "defect"[68] that needs to be wiped out, and sometimes they are seen as "gifts"[69] or happy irregularities. In Christian language, some of these mutations are seen as resulting from the Fall (the soul misprogramming the body via its DNA), and some of these mutations are seen as resulting from God's design (God enjoying, as with race, good diversity and so puts diversity into the soul's original programming).

In recent years especially, some *X-Men* stories have been used to discuss

---

66  The soul's programming of the body via DNA is generally according to God's design, but some of this has been damaged by the Fall. Hermaphrodites or intersexed persons, for example, are people born with an ambiguous sex, which on my model could not result from an ambiguous gender since a person has essentially one and only gender. In their case, something likely has gone wrong with the soul-to-body programming, and the body remains in a broken or disabled state as a result.
67  *Astonishing X-Men: Ultimate Collection* vol. 1.
68  The villain Phalanx sees all particularities, including mutant abilities, as defects that need eliminating. *X-Men: The Animated Series* season 5, episode 2.
69  Professor X, for example, calls his mutant academy "Xavier's School for Gifted Youngsters."

societal attitudes toward homosexuals, usually showing that those who see homosexual orientation / the mutant condition as a defect or disability to be ignorant and dangerous (William Stryker and the Purifiers, for example[70]) and those who see it as a good or God-designed thing to be in the right (the X-Men). Thus, when Emma Frost hears that there is a geneticist who wants to eliminate the mutant X-gene, she remarks coldly, "What's next? Eliminating the gay gene?"[71] What's interesting here is the double claim that (1) homosexual orientation is undeniably linked to one's biological programming, and (2) all things linked to one's biological programming are good "gifts." Connected with these two claims is often the additional claim that (3) this biological "gift" of sexual orientation is intimately connected with one's identity. None of these claims, however, are very accurate.

To begin with, sexual orientation—the erotic disposition toward a particular sex—is probably a thing of this world, and not, like gender, one of the next. In the New Earth, we will almost certainly retain our gender and thus our gender duties and relations—marriage may even still exist for some— yet given what Jesus said about "being like the angels" (who usually have no biological, and hence sexed, bodies), it seems less likely that we'll have a sex much less a sexual orientation. Thus, sexual orientation, even heterosexual orientation, which all Christians claim to be a good and God-designed thing, will probably not exist for us.

Yet while from a metaphysical point-of-view sexual orientation isn't likely to constitute an important part of one's identity, isn't it an important part of one's physical identity at least? Isn't "the gay gene" proof of this? The problem here is that pace Emma Frost no one has found a gay gene. In 1991 neuroscientist Simon LeVay, himself a gay man, announced he had discovered a gay gene, yet in subsequent years, he was disproved to the point where in 1994, LeVay himself admitted, "It's important to stress what I didn't find. I did not prove that homosexuality was genetic, or find a genetic cause for being gay."[72]

Now certainly some with a homosexual orientation share some unique chromosomal markers with each other, especially chromosome Xq28. But this is neither necessary nor sufficient to show that these markers *cause* homosexuality since there are those with a homosexual orientation who don't have these markers, and there are those with a heterosexual orientation who have these markers.[73] These markers don't cause one's sexual orientation, but

---

70  See *X-Men: God Loves, Man Kills*.
71  *Astonishing X-Men: Ultimate Collection* vol. 1.
72  Simon LeVay cited in David Nimmons, "Sex and the Brain," *Discover* 15, no. 3 (1994): 64-71.
73  Stanton Jones and Mark Yarhouse, *Homosexuality: The Use of Scientific Research in*

may play a part in shaping one's temperament—a temperament which could, more easily than other temperaments, incline one toward a homosexual orientation if other factors were also introduced. Nevertheless, even this has been challenged.

What's more, chromosome Xq28 is not obviously good in and of itself. While it's certainly possible—even probable in the absence of clear evidence to the contrary—that the temperament produced by chromosome Xq28 is part of God's design and thus this chromosome is something He wanted the soul to program into the DNA, it's still possible that it's a form of biological brokenness, similar to the biological brokenness of cancer cells, stemming from the Fall. This is to say that being born with a thing is no guarantee that that thing is a "gift" or a part of God's original good design. When Jesus was asked who sinned such that the blind man was born blind, He replied, "Neither this man nor his parents . . . but this happened so that the work of God might be displayed in his life."[74] Now this is surely true; it is surely true that God used this man's blindness or disability to work virtue in the man and glorify God therein. However, I think it likely that God only used blindness as a means to teach the man virtue (and so to glorify God) in the first place because brokenness was already introduced into creation by Adam's original sin. In other words, if man hadn't fallen, then it seems unlikely that God would have used clear badness to teach us goodness since we probably could have learned virtue, and God could have been glorified therein, without such obvious badness. The X-Men, for example, can develop their skills in the Danger Room without actually posing any real risk to their person.

The key thing to take note of is that *some* homosexuals might have their sexual orientation *partially influenced* by a temperament *partially grounded* in their biology, just as *some* smokers might have their smoking habit *partially influenced* by a temperament *partially grounded* in some of their biology. But this is a far cry from a gay gene that causes a person to be gay, and it certainly is a far cry from saying that this hypothetical gene is good. Indeed, because both special revelation (the Bible)[75] and general revelation (the Natural Law)[76] seem

---

*the Church's Moral Debate* (Downers Grove, IL: IVP, 2000), 80-81.
74  John 9:2-3.
75  "The list of verses that directly address the subject of homosexual behavior is only six to eight long, depending on how you define direct. But the passages that do address homosexual behavior speak with one voice on the subject and are *crystal clear in condemning homosexual behavior, male and female, every time it is mentioned.*" Jones and Yarhouse, *Homosexuality*, 20. See esp. 1 Corinthians 6:9-11.
76  Although homosexual practices can be found in many global cultures, its condemnation is also nearly as universal. For example, although Plato lived in a culture where homosexual behavior wasn't uncommon, the Father of Philosophy still

to speak so clearly denouncing freely-entered-into homosexual *acts* or *behavior* as sin or injustice, it's likely that the orientation or disposition that inclines one toward these acts is bad—bad, not sin; but still, bad as cancer is bad, or bad as the inclination to love comic books more than God is bad. *Marvel 1602*'s Angel might be right when he says he's not a "monster" in respect to his wings, but certainly, if the monstrous means something like "against God's good design," then Angel's attraction to Jean Grey, who he thought was a boy, *is* monstrous.

But if genetics don't come close to explaining any homosexual orientation completely, and some, not at all,[77] what other factors might help explain this disabling orientation?

Environmental factors (too many to mention here) can play a part—but again, not necessarily cause—this orientation. One study shows that men and women who experienced sexual abuse as children were three times more likely to report a homosexual orientation than those who didn't experience sexual abuse as children. Another study found that 58% of boys who were sexually abused considered themselves gay or bisexual, but 90% of boys who were not abused thought of themselves as heterosexual.[78] Even with more indirect abuse, this sort of phenomenon occurs. For example, boys raised without fathers or raised by emotionally unavailable fathers are more likely to develop a homosexual orientation than boys with loving fathers.[79]

Here we should pause to note the importance of a father or a father-figure in modeling and encouraging correct behavior in his son. Bruce Wayne, we are told, has been a moral "compass" for his wards and now his son, Damian, meaning that Bruce has taught them, through both words and deeds, what it means to be a good man.[80] More specifically, in respect to the soul and the

---

recognized that this behavior is "unnatural," which is to say, unjust or against the universal moral principles of the Natural Law. Plato *Laws* 839. Or again in Thailand, Thai Theravada Buddhism maintains, "Homosexuality arises as a karmic consequence of violating Buddhist proscriptions against heterosexual misconduct in a previous incarnation." Peter Jackson, "Thai Buddhist Accounts of Male Homosexuality and AIDS in the 1980s," *The Australian Journal of Anthropology* 6, no. 3 (December 1995): 140–153.

77  Richard Friedman and Jennifer Downey, *Sexual Orientation and Psychoanalysis: Sexual Science and Clinical Practice* (New York: Columbia University Press, 2002), 39.

78  Edward Lauman et al., *The Social Organization of Sexuality: Sexual Practices in the United States* (Chicago: University of Chicago Press, 1994), 344.

79  Glenn Stanton and Bill Maier, *Marriage on Trial: The Case against Same-Sex Marriage and Parenting* (Downers Groove, IL: IVP, 2004), 136.

80  *Batman and Robin: Born to Kill*. A father, of course, must also teach his daughter what it means to be a good woman, but here the task includes, among other things, showing the daughter what the masculine is so that she can respond to it correctly

masculine gender, what this would mean is that Bruce has taught his son how to act manly, which is to say, how to treat the feminine gender justly, and in respect to the body and male sexuality, what this would mean is that Bruce has taught his son how to direct his sexual desires and behavior in ways in keeping with justice. Bruce, in other words, has not taught his son how to be "statistically normal" (as pro-gay philosophers might say) but rather how to be just.

Social factors of all sorts can also play a part—but again, not cause—a homosexual orientation. Fredric Wertham was wrong about many things, but he wasn't wrong about "socialization" in general, which is to say he wasn't wrong to say we tend to become like the things we surround ourselves with. Wertham was wrong to think Batman gay and Wonder Woman a lesbian,[81] but he wouldn't have been wrong to be concerned about them *if* they were, in fact, heroes endorsing a gay lifestyle. I certainly agree that since homosexual acts are morally bad and a homosexual orientation is non-morally bad, the subsequent Comics Code was wise to forbid "sexual abnormalities."[82] Indeed, I'd wager to say that since 1989, when the Code was revised, allowing a homosexual lifestyle to be "portrayed in a positive light,"[83] comic book readers have been affected for the worse. Indeed, with DC transforming Batwoman from an early love-interest of Batman's to a full-on lesbian, or making Alan Scott, the first Green Lantern, a "brave, mighty and gay" superhero in the New 52 universe,[84] the goodness of superheroes has decreased, and so, I expect, has its positive influence on readers. And this is especially true with Marvel's "wedding" between Alpha Flight's Northstar and his boyfriend, Kyle Jinadu.[85]

Gay marriage clearly doesn't fit with the Christian view of marriage, which is a monogamous relationship between only one man and only one woman,[86] nor does it help men and women to flourish in respect to their genders: it doesn't help teach men to pursue, protect and lead women, nor

---

as the feminine. Commissioner Gordon, for example, seems to have done a good job of this since his daughter, Batgirl, thinks thus: "Every daughter wants her dad to be a white knight. Every daughter wants her father to be Lancelot." *Batgirl: Knightfall Descends*.
81  Madrid, *The Supergirls*, 51, 55.
82  Nyberg, *Seal of Approval*, 143.
83  Ibid., 175-176.
84  In *Earth-2: The Gathering*, Alan Scott was re-launched as a "brave, mighty, and gay" Green Lantern. http://entertainment.ca.msn.com/celebs/green-lantern-relaunched-as-brave-mighty-and-gay-1
85  *Astonishing X-Men* vol. 1, #51. In the *Young Justice* TV series, Martian Manhunter's niece, Megan, dates Superboy. The problem with this is that she is asexual, meaning that if she were to marry Superboy, we'd have a problematic marriage here as well.
86  Matthew 19:3-7.

women to submit, strengthen and ennoble men. Yet because only about 2-3% of the population of North America is in fact gay, and maybe only a quarter of these would want to get married (maybe .5% of the total population), we might think that showing gay marriage in a positive light would have little effect on people. Perhaps so; but perhaps not. Things that show homosexuality—either the orientation or acts themselves—as positive could be cited as potential reasons to stop opposing many who could be saved from a homosexual lifestyle, or could be cited as a factor, along with other factors such as biological or environmental ones, in a homosexual orientation taking root.

Nevertheless, all of this has been to speak of a homosexual orientation as a disability that simply develops independently of a person's own choice.[87] Here we must remember that one of the disabling effects of the Fall is that human desires and emotions are, to some degree, in rebellion against reason, which is the faculty that discerns good and evil. Often we *want* what is unjust even though we *know* what is just. So even though I do think that most who have a homosexual orientation never imagined themselves wanting to be gay or choosing to have the orientation they have; nevertheless, with enough biological, environmental and social factors, plus a heart generally inclined to injustice, a person could come to convince himself or herself that a homosexual orientation is a gift that needs to be celebrated and exercised, rather than a disabling disposition that needs to be struggled against and—if not in this life,[88] at least in the next life—cured. Thus, while Alpha Flight's Aurora could say it more tactfully, she isn't wrong to want to see her brother, Northstar's, "sick obsession with men . . . removed."[89]

---

[87] Although the American Psychiatric Association's *Diagnostic and Statistical Manual of Mental Disorders* removed homosexual orientation from its official list of mental disorders in 1973, this was mostly a political move, rather than a medical one, and certainly relevant Christian experts wouldn't agree with this removal. See Ronald Bayer, *Homosexuality and American Psychiatry: The Politics of Diagnosis* (New York: Basic Books, 1981), 39-40.

[88] This is to say that people with a homosexual orientation must not engage in homosexual acts, which are always unjust, and should also try to remove this orientation. That this orientation can be removed to some degree in some people is clear. See R. L. Spitzer, "Can Some Gay Men and Lesbians Change Their Orientation? 200 Participants Reporting a Change from Homosexual to Heterosexual Orientation," *Archives of Sexual Behavior* 32, no. 5 (2003): 403-417. However, in this life the removal of this orientation is hard, and some who have it may never succeed in removing it, just as some, even well-intending ones, might not fully succeed in overcoming smoking, porn addiction, or such things. The healing work of Christ doesn't work the same in all, and so some healing will need to be completed in the next life. St. Paul asked Christ to take away his "thorn in the flesh," but it wasn't taken away in this life. 2 Corinthians 12:7-10.

[89] *Alpha Flight: The Complete Series* (2012).

## CONCLUSION

In this chapter, I tried to show how gender, gender duties and disabilities relating to gender, especially homosexual orientation, are portrayed in superhero mythology. In respect to gender, I argued that masculinity and femininity are properties in the soul that help determine, if relevant, the sex of the body. In the DC and Marvel universes, God is typically depicted as masculine, which agrees with orthodox Christianity, and while Marvel and DC both gender-bend a few of their characters, such as Loki and Martian Manhunter, for the most part, most of their major characters have one gender and possess this gender consistently, which is the biblical model.

This consistency is important, moreover, because each gender—the masculine and the feminine—come with different moral obligations toward each other. The masculine is to pursue, protect and lead the feminine—to act manly—whereas the feminine is to receive, support and build up the worthy masculine—to act womanly. While by and large most superheroes do act in keeping with their genders, some problems do arise. There are a few superheroes who don't know how to both act in keeping with their gender *and* be heroic, but most, especially the earlier superheroes, do. Additionally, while most of the earlier superheroes were strongly grounded in general moral principles—the health of all good mythology—some of the more recent superheroes have in fact compromised some of their goodness by partaking in, or at least supporting, injustices such as sex before marriage, immodesty in dress, and, most recently, homosexual acts and gay marriage.

Nevertheless, while I needed to highlight some problematic cases for study, for the most part, superhero mythology is healthy, and its gender portrayals are positive. And it certainly should give us hope that in a world where immorality, including gender immorality, is popular—in a world where, in the words of Green Arrow, "Pirates are sexy and hit men kick-ass"[90]—there are still persons who lament the calling of "bad" "good" and fight to change this.

---

90 *Green Arrow: The Midas Touch.*

# CHAPTER THREE

## Superman: From Anti-Christ to Christ-Type

Although the Roman poet Lucian was probably the first to speak of a "super-man" or *hyperanthropos*, the term was popularized and entered the English language from the writings of the German philologist and philosopher Friedrich Nietzsche, who spoke of an *übermensch*. For Nietzsche, this word was a positive one, denoting a man whose ethics were "beyond good and evil," a man who had the "courage" to reject traditional morality in order to forge his own unrestricted destiny. Yet, English speakers who first encountered the word "super-man" were largely Judeo-Christians, who for the most part believed in a universal moral law, which meant that for them, the Nietzschean word "super-man" was unqualifiedly negative. But something happened between then and now that has rehabilitated the word "super-man," not as a recovery of the Nietzschean sense, but rather of the diametrically opposed sense, a Judeo-Christian sense. That thing—that event—was the advent of DC's Superman, who, I will show, was created quite intentionally to subvert Nietzsche's *übermensch*.

To substantiate this I will argue that the rehabilitation of the word "super-man" was intentional, yet what resulted was far more than the original authors dreamt of. The super-man in the works of Nietzsche and the first story by Siegel and Shuster is a literal antichrist, yet this man becomes, through gradual changes over the years, nothing less than a Christ-type par excellence. Thus, what started out subjective became the herald of what is objective; what began with power directed to amoral self-actualization became power directed toward the betterment of others; what was once the mad prophet decrying the death of God is now the greatest modern symbol of Immanuel, God-With-Us.

### *ÜBERMENSCH* AS ANTICHRIST

Friedrich Nietzsche espoused a particular form of moral relativism, asserting four key things.

First, he rightly accepted the fact of cultural relativism, namely that different cultures often reach different moral conclusions. This claim is, as I said, a fact and is asserted by people as diverse as Plato, Lao Tzu, Thomas Aquinas and the Buddha. However, Nietzsche coupled this objective fact with a more dubious argument. He thought the greatest German philosopher, Immanuel Kant, hadn't gone far enough in his theorizing insofar as Kant still dogmatically asserted the existence of certain objective truths, in particular, logical truths (the Law of Contradiction), mathematical truths (1 + 1 = 2) and moral truths ("It's always wrong to torture a child for fun"). Leaping logic in a single bound, Nietzsche oddly argued that cultural diversity and dogmatic assertions for objectivity prove that there is no objectivity, in particular no universal moral law or objective norms that all cultures can know.

Second, accepting the Judeo-Christian argument linking the universal moral law and God (that is, the argument that shows God is identical to the Good), Nietzsche went on to proclaim the non-existence of the Almighty, which for him became the cornerstone of his philosophy: "Beyond question the major premise of Nietzsche's philosophy is atheism."[1]

Third, Nietzsche thought the loss of God would result in global madness because the death of Deity is connected to the death of objective norms, stable aesthetic values, proper emotional responses to such norms and values, and, last but not least, human dignity (since this would mean man is no longer made in the image of God). Nietzsche's philosophy is often called "nihilism" because it preaches the need to wake up to the fact of such barren nothingness.

And fourth, only the person who realizes that norms and values are nothing but human constructs is able, though by no means guaranteed to, become a new, superior type of man, the *übermensch* or super-man. That is, because Nietzsche believed living in any kind of illusion is objectively bad (we might agree but this is ironic for a denouncer of objective morality), he thought the super-man needs an unwavering desire to be free from the "social construct" that is objective morality, in particular, Judeo-Christian morality. Furthermore, accepting the near universal claim that people desire happiness but insisting, controversially, that happiness actually means "power," Nietzsche thought the "super-man," no less than a mere man, would have a will to, or desire for, power, yet the super-man would distinguish himself from a mere man by desiring power in a way that is free from all moral and social constraints. In short, he wouldn't worry about what others say is "good" or "bad" but would, by his own genius and creativity, construct his own norms in order to create for himself a persona of his choosing. The super-man would thus revile such "non-Aryan" (that is, Judeo-Christian rather than Germanic pagan[2]) virtues as pity and mercy, since these would distract the super-man from his own goals

---

1   George Morgan, *What Nietzsche Means* (Cambridge: Harvard University Press, 1941), 36.
2   Friedrich Nietzsche *Twilight of the Idols* 7.4.

of self-actualization. True, the super-man thrives on conflict and challenge; however, the super-man won't thrive, as the Judeo-Christian tradition has maintained, by the challenge of helping the pitiable or anonymous weak since the sense of power that the super-man would get from helping the weak is power that is dependent on conforming to society's arbitrary moral standards and thus is to take part in an illusion. To most of society, then, the super-man will be a kind of antichrist (the title of one of Nietzsche's books), not insofar as his primary goal is to hurt and deceive others (the weak think thus) but rather insofar as he hurts others "without thinking"—as a byproduct or the inevitable result of self-creation: "The truly powerful are not concerned with others but act out of fullness and an overflow."[3] We can see, then, that Jesus, for example, is far from Nietzsche's super-man ideal, for though the Christ strove under challenge, he lacked clarity about the proper purpose of such striving: Jesus was, in the words of Nietzsche, "a case of delayed . . . puberty."[4]

## SUPER-MAN AS LEX LUTHOR

During World War I, "Feelings ran high both in Germany, where [Nietzsche's] *Zarathustra* was pushed to new sales records as a 'must' for the soldier's knapsack, and in England and the United States, where Nietzsche began to be considered the apostle of German ruthlessness and barbarism. . . . During those war years, the 'superman' began to be associated with the German nation."[5] This feeling in America was intensified during World War II with "the advent of Hitler and the Nazis' brazen adaptation of Nietzsche."[6] So, while Nietzsche himself was surprisingly neither a proponent of German nationalism nor a racist (he calls himself an "anti-anti-Semite"[7]), the English speaking world, though especially those in America, tended to see him as the unofficial philosopher of the Nazis.

In 1933, when Hitler—himself fuelled by a slight misunderstanding of Nietzsche's super-man—started to dream of world domination, Jewish American cartoonists Jerry Siegel and Joe Shuster co-wrote a short story for *Science Fiction* #3 called "The Reign of the Super-Man." The use of the word "Super-Man" was a clear allusion to Nietzsche, though it depicted Nietzsche's super-man as a bald megalomaniac bent on global conquest. Certainly, if famed German psychologist Fredric Wertham had in mind *this* Super-Man when he claimed the Man of Steel is a fascist who "undermines the authority

---

3   Walter Kaufmann, *Nietzsche: Philosopher, Psychologist, Antichrist*, 4th edition (Princeton: Princeton University Press, 1974), 194.
4   Friedrich Nietzsche *The Anti-Christ* 32.
5   Kaufmann, *Nietzsche: Philosopher, Psychologist, Antichrist*, 8.
6   Ibid., 9.
7   Ibid., 44.

and dignity of . . . ordinary men and women,"[8] we could easily see his point. Here, Super-Man is a proto-Lex Luthor, and Lex Luthor was what Siegel and Shuster thought Nietzsche and Hitler were all about. And by making Super-Man a villain, Siegel and Shuster clearly, and rightly, intended to subvert Nietzsche's savage super-man.

This understanding, of course, only gets Nietzsche partially right, for though Nietzsche's super-man does indeed crave power and is in fact willing to sacrifice whatever it takes to achieve power, the power he craves is more for self-actualization and absolute freedom of will than it is for world domination (even if world domination could arguably be an expression or entailment of these). Nietzsche's super-man, in other words, is more nuanced than Hitler or Siegel and Shuster's Super-Man, yet all three share the same distaste, even hatred, for Judeo-Christian morality, in particular, pity, mercy and sacrificial love.

## JESUS WITHOUT THE CHRIST

In 1938, five years after his debut yet still during wartime, the Super-Man became Superman. In *Action Comics* vol. 1, #1, Superman was re-envisioned as nearly the opposite of the Nietzschean, antichrist Super-Man. Rather than let a perfectly good word like "superman" be associated with Nietzsche, Hitler and Lex Luthor, it was intentionally redeemed, though it remained subversive. While still strong and determined like the Nietzschean Super-Man, Superman became a hero of the Judeo-Christian sort: he accepted the principles of the universal moral law, in particular, concern for the weak, without question and never failed to act in accordance with these laws. Moreover, even if Siegel and Shuster intentionally made some parallels between Superman and Moses, such as them both being sent away from their parents only for them to become great heroes,[9] the parallels between Superman and another Jew—a more famous Jew—are much more striking.[10]

Jesus, who Siegel and Shuster must have taken special pride in calling a Jew and who Christians believe is the Son of, and indeed one with, Elohim or God the Father, was, at least on the level of myth and morality, the figure behind the creation of Superman.[11] Some of this was very intentional

---

8   Grant Morrison, *Supergods: What Masked Vigilantes, Miraculous Mutants, and a Sun God from Smallville Can Teach Us about Being Human* (New York: Spiegel & Grau, 2012), 55.
9   Howard Jacobson, "Up, Up and Oy Vey," *The Times*, March 5, 2005.
10  I'm not the first person to have noticed these parallels. For instance, see Stephen Skelton, *The Gospel According to the World's Greatest Hero* (Eugene, OR: Harvest House, 2006) and John Wesley White, *The Man from Krypton: The Gospel According to Superman* (Minneapolis, MN: Bethany Fellowship, 1978).
11  Jesus isn't the only famous biblical hero to be alluded to, or make an appearance

and explicit. For instance, in *Superman Comics* vol. 1, #1 the Man of Steel's adoptive mother, Martha Kent, was originally named *Mary*, and his adoptive father, named in a latter issue, is Jonathan *Joseph* Kent. Though this allusion would later become obscured by changing "Mary" to "Martha" (or, rather, by introducing the concept of multiverses), the allusion to the Holy Family—who, we should nevertheless remember, are constantly depicted as church-going Christians[12]—reappears again with a vengeance in *Smallville*, when Martha, reworking St. John's "not that we loved God but that He loved us,"[13] says of young Kal-El, "We didn't find him; he found us."[14]

However, some of the connections between Superman and Jesus were only loosely made. Consider two examples, both having to do with names.

First, "Clark" in "Clark Kent" means "cleric" or "priest" and "Kent" is a form of the Hebrew word *kana*, which, in its *k-n-t* form, appears in the Bible, meaning "I have found a son." Thus, "Clark Kent" could mean "I have found a son, a priest," which could very well be an allusion to Jesus, who is called the True Priest. Yet even more strikingly, another derivation of the word *kana* is the Greek word *krista* or our English word "Christ." For those who think this is a stretch (I was one of them), we'd do well to remember that the word "Krypton" is from the Greek word *kryptos* or "hidden"—Krypton, Superman's home planet, being "hidden" from us on Earth. Thus it seems that either way "Clark Kent" was far from an arbitrary name, being intended to denote a priest or a savior.

Second, some years later, Superman's real name was revealed to be Kal-El and his biological father, Jor-El. *El* is the Hebrew word meaning "(of) God" (such as in *El*ohim), which makes it clear that with this name as well there is a strong connection—both mythically in terms of being a divine figure, and morally in terms of acting righteously—between God and Superman. Joined with the word *el* is the word *kal*, which in Hebrew means "vessel." Thus, we have the idea that Superman is a "vessel of God."[15] Indeed, even years later,

---

in, *Superman* comics. Shazam has the wisdom of King Solomon and the biblical Samson is an on-again-off-again friend of the Man of Steel. See *Superman's Pal, Jimmy Olson* vol. 1, #16 (October 1956) and *All-Star Superman*. Additionally, the demons Satanus, Beliala and Beelzebub are mentioned as real characters in the DC universe, and Superman encounters villains named Gog and Magog, Cain and Abel, and Sodom and Gomorrah, not to mention a former priest-turned-monster named Pilate. Even in *Smallville*, Darkseid is identified as "Lucifer." *Smallville* season 10, episode 21.

12   *Action Comics* vol. 1, #848 (May 2007).
13   1 John 4:10.
14   *Smallville* season 1, episode 1.
15   David Lewis, "Superman Graveside: Superhero Salvation beyond Jesus," in *Graven Images: Religion in Comic Books and Graphic Novels*, ed. A. David Lewis and

when the Hebrew word *el* is explained to be actually a Kryptonian word, the divine connotations aren't completely lost, for if the Kryptonian "el" means "child" and "kal" means "star," then "Kal-El," like Jesus, whose birth was heralded by the Star of Bethlehem, is also a "star-child."[16]

Yet if we return to the Hebrew word, we should note, in fairness, that *el* need not imply identity with God (as in *El*ohim) but could simply suggest service to God and His righteousness (as with the helper angel Gabri*el*). Moreover, that Superman was initially depicted performing local acts of justice, such as stopping wife beaters, gangsters and so on, and often in a very rough, non-idealized way, suggests that Superman was at this stage more like an angel (in later comics he is called "an angel sent straight from Heaven"[17]) or Jesus the healer and priest than a cosmic Christ. Thus, though both Jesus's and Superman's local acts of healing and heroics should be seen as representative of their pure hearts and devotion to even the lowliest (and in this sense philosopher Umberto Eco is wrong for thinking these are a "waste of means"), such acts, *at least by themselves*, aren't the acts of a great mythical hero.[18] Consequently, although already both a direct challenge to Nietzsche's ideal and an important step in semantic change, Superman was only a partial Christ-type when he was re-envisioned in the 1930s.

## MORAL ILLUMINATION

A short while later, two new elements were added to Superman's mythology that further distinguished the Man of Steel as a Christ-type.

The first had to do with Superman's powers. Although Superman's powers were first explained to be the result of advanced Kryptonian evolution, they were later understood to be caused by the Earth's yellow sun. This had nothing to do with science or the evolution vs. creationism debates of the time. Rather, it had to do with substituting a poor myth for a more potent one. Superman's reliance on the yellow sun had nuances of Christ's reliance on God the Father, who's metaphorically, and cross-religiously, I should add, spoken of as the Sun. Indeed, there aren't many better metaphors for truth and justice than the Sun, which means that the Superman myth, here, takes a sharp turn upward.

The second had to do with Superman's absolute code against killing. During the early years of superheroes, there was a tremendous amount of social pressure to censor comics. One of the results was that DC instituted a code that prevented any of its heroes from killing, and, in true Aristotelian

---

Christine Kraemer (London: Continuum, 2010), 180.
16   *Superman's Pal, Jimmy Olson* vol. 1, #121 (July 1969).
17   *Superman* vol. 1, #657 (February 2007).
18   Umberto Eco, "The Myth of Superman," in *The Role of the Reader: Explorations in the Semiotics of Text* (n.p.: First Midland, 1984), 123.

fashion, made it mandatory that good always triumphs over evil (where good and evil were understood from the universal moral perspective, which is in keeping with Judeo-Christian concepts of truth and justice). Of course from the point of view of DC, this was just good business, but from the point of view of comic book lovers, the result was a deepened sense that superheroes are moral absolutists.

Of course, there are enormous problems for those who think that killing is *absolutely* wrong or wrong under all circumstances. What if a person was about to murder your child and you had the choice to kill the would-be murderer or let your child be killed? What would you do? More importantly, what is the *right* or *just* thing to do given the universal moral law? While most agree that it's *generally* wrong to kill people, the duty against killing needs to be qualified by other duties, such as the duty to save innocent persons from being murdered. Thus, killing the would-be murderer might not only *feel* right but might also *be* right.

Now although Superman does occasionally tackle some tough moral scenarios having to do with his code against killing, most of the scenarios are relatively easy compared to the one I just mentioned. For example, when Superman actually did execute some homicidal criminals from the Phantom Zone, he quickly came to the conclusion that because he had the strength not to kill them, he was wrong to do so.[19] Here we might all agree, especially since Superman isn't necessarily a lawful authority who can lawfully carry forth capital punishment. Or again, in one episode of *The Justice League*, Superman is faced with the choice of killing Mongul's henchman Prega or keeping his own chains on and then being beaten to a pulp; Superman keeps them on until the fight is declared over, at which point he easily breaks them and says, quoting Jesus, to Prega, who asked why he hadn't broken them earlier, "It's called 'turning the other cheek.'"[20] Though this situation also isn't easy, probably the best of us would admire Superman for sticking to a non-killing version of Jesus's apparent personal pacifism.[21] Or finally, on another occasion, Superman was being mind-controlled by Maxwell Lord such that the *only* way the Man of Steel could be freed was for Lord to die. Wonder Woman, out of a sense of justice, killed Lord and set Superman free, but far from being grateful, Superman said on a later occasion, "Only the weak succumb to brutality."[22] Personally, I think Wonder Woman acted rightly, but Superman could also be seen as right insofar as Wonder Woman should have known that he would

---

19  *Superman* vol. 2, #28 (February 1989).
20  *The Justice League* season 1, episode 12.
21  I say "apparent" since I'm not convinced that Jesus espoused pacifism in even this narrow sense.
22  *Kingdom Come*. Cf. *The Adventures of Superman* vol. 1, #642 (September 2005).

rather have been a slave than see Lord's neck broken. While not an easy case, it's easy compared to, say, a situation where Superman would have to kill a would-be murderer to save Lois, or even if he had the choice to either shoot down the airplanes heading for the World Trade Center (killing all aboard) or letting the planes hit (killing all on board and those in the buildings). Not yet faced with such a dilemma, Superman remains adamant that killing rational creatures is murder, plain and simple, though I hasten to add in his defense that most killings would, in fact, probably be murder for *him* since he does have the power to do otherwise, while we human beings usually don't.

Thus, if taken seriously as an ethical position, Superman's absolute code against killing is hard to maintain, not to mention, admire. Yet because Superman's inflexibility came to be seen more generally as a symbol of moral integrity—a sign that Superman is willing to do whatever he can to simultaneously keep all moral commands at once, rather than weigh one against another—he became a kind of perfect moral ideal . . . as Christ was and is.[23] Thus, it's not his actual belief that killing is wrong that made him a Christ-type, so much as his unshakable moral convictions and refusal to compromise what he believes is right. "The world changed," Magog tells Superman, "but you wouldn't."[24]

Consequently, Superman's absolute devotion to the universal moral law and Judeo-Christian morality stands in stark contrast to Nietzschean power morality. Nietzsche says, "If you have such a boring and ugly object in yourself, by all means do think more of others than of yourself."[25] But Superman agrees with an old lady who says, "Some of true faith know in their heart the simple difference between helpin' others or just helpin' themselves."[26] Where Nietzsche sees sacrificial love as a weakness because it conforms to social standards, Superman, offering up his very soul to the demon Satanus in exchange for the souls of Metropolites,[27] sees sacrificial love as strength insofar as such conforms to the highest law. Nietzsche's super-man thinks himself brave for rejecting notions like forgiveness, but is thus aligned with the villain Lex Luthor, who, Superman says, "doesn't have the *courage* to change" because he can't overlook an insult.[28] Nietzsche might agree with the phrasing of *The Essential Superman Encyclopedia* when it says, "Enemies preyed upon [Superman's] moral code,

---

23 Similarly, Leo Braudy says that Superman "comes the closest to embodying Plato's idea of the Good." Leo Braudy, "The Mythology of Superman," in *You Will Believe: The Cinematic Saga of Superman* (Warner Bros., 2006).
24 *Kingdom Come*. Superman is also famous for never telling a lie. See *Superman: Grounded* vol. 1.
25 Friedrich Nietzsche *The Dawn* 131.
26 *Action Comics* vol. 1, #849 (July 2007).
27 *Action Comics* vol. 1, #832 (October 2005).
28 *Action Comics* vol. 1, #900 (June 2011).

turning it into a weakness;"[29] yet love is only a weakness if one thinks that true strength or happiness means, as Nietzsche would have it, caring only, or primarily, about one's self. As a result, Nietzsche's thoughts are shown to be like Bizarro's, which are dark and counterintuitive, and the Skeptic's, which doubt the readily discernable,[30] but Superman's are shown to be illuminated by the heavenly rays of truth and justice.

## KRYPTO, COMET AND A STEP BACKWARDS

Of course, to see Superman as a Christ-type does require a bit of picking and choosing. There are certainly elements along the way that don't help my argument, though these elements mostly have to do with mythical resonance.

Krypto the Superdog, Comet the Superhorse and Streaky the Supercat are three such instances. These, not to mention Supergirl, Superboy and the Kandorians, tend to diminish Superman's most mythical title, "The Last Son of Krypton." This title has great mythical weight not only because, as I said, the word *kryptos* is the Greek word for "hidden" or "secret" but mostly because the word "last" coveys the sense of uniqueness and wonder—wonder of some ancient mystery hidden, only to be hinted at or revealed in this one final person. Jesus is *the* Son of God, not *a* son of God: He is the connection to the great hidden mystery that is God, Our Origin. If there were more than one Jesus—more than one messiah who could bridge the way between God and man—then His importance would be reduced, and with it, His gravitas. The same is true of Superman. Krypto, Comet and Streaky might help sell comics, but only at the cost of trivializing the myth of Superman.

## TRINITARIAN MOVIE MYTHOS

While *Superman* comics during the '50s, '60s and '70s often had little in the way of *numinous* or mythical and moral *gravitas*, the first two *Superman* movies—*Superman: The Movie* (1978) and *Superman II* (1981)—played important roles in furthering the Man of Tomorrow's role as a Christ-type.

In these movies Superman is no longer merely Jesus the healer, priest and moral exemplar, but is now clearly depicted as a Son-of-God-type. In *Superman: The Movie*, Jor-El is a God-figure sending his only begotten son to become the savior of a world: "Even though you've been raised as a human being, you're not one of them," he tells his son, "They can be great people, Kal-El, if they wish to be. They only lack the light to show the way. For this reason, above all, their capacity for good, I have sent them you, my only son."

---

29 Robert Greenberger and Martin Pasko, *The Essential Superman Encyclopedia* (New York: Del Rey, 2010), 405.
30 *World's Finest Comics* vol. 1, #11 (Fall 1942).

## Imitating the Saints

And such connections in the movie don't stop there: both Jesus and Superman were raised incognito on Earth, both began their mission at the age of thirty, both try—at least for a while—to hide their identities, both assume self-imposed servitude, and, among a myriad of other examples,[31] both fulfill prophecies; for instance, in *Superman II*, when Jor-El restores Superman's powers, and by doing so, exhausts his own, we are told, "The Kryptonian prophecy will at last be fulfilled: the son becomes the father and the father becomes the son"—Superman embraces the vision of his father and his father fills his son, Superman, with the power to achieve his vision. Here we have the first, though not the last, example of Trinitarian symbolism in Superman mythology.

## DEATH AND RETURN

Superman is an *American* myth. This is important in its own way (as philosopher A. C. Grayling has pointed out[32]), but it's not important as *myth* per se. All the great myths, insofar as they are great, have a universality about them. The Americana, in other words, is peripheral to the myth itself.

In *Superman II*, the Man of Steel still fights for "Truth, Justice and the American Way," but he also takes the first step beyond this toward becoming a world savior: when General Zod and his lackeys uproot and discard both the American and Soviet flags planted on the Moon, it's a symbol of Zod threatening the entire planet. Consequently, Superman can no longer remain a domestic hero, but now must become an international, indeed, a cosmic, hero as well.

This cosmic idea grew throughout the '80s, '90s and beyond, such that in *The Brightest Day* vol. 2, Superman declares that he fights for "Truth, Justice and the Universal Way" and in *Action Comics* vol. 1, #900, Superman even renounces his U. S. citizenship, not because he doesn't love America, but because he, quite properly, loves the values particular to America less than he loves the values universally shared.

At the box office, the 2006 movie *Superman Returns* follows, and expands on, this trend, dropping the "American way" part of the phrase. In this movie, Superman is stripped of his cultural particularities (which may have had something to do with movie's poor domestic box office gross), yet becomes, in the words of its director, Bryan Singer, "The Jesus Christ of Superheroes"[33]

---

31  See Anton Kozlovic, "Superman as Christ-Figure: The American Pop Culture Movie Messiah," *Journal of Religion and Film* 6, no. 1 (April 2002).
32  A. C. Grayling, "The Philosophy of Superman: A Short Course," *The Spectator*, July 8, 2006.
33  Bryan Singer, quoted in "The Spiritual Side of *Superman Returns*" by Stephen Skelton, *SuperHeroHype.com*, December 4, 2006, http://www.superherohype.com/

(which may have had something to do with the movie's better-than-expected international—that is, universal—box office gross).[34]

In this movie, parallels between Superman and Christ are everywhere, though six in particular are worth mentioning: (1) the movie begins with Superman saving a shuttle named Genesis; (2) later, from a God's eye perspective of the world, Superman tells the disenchanted Lois Lane, who denies hearing anything from up there, "[You hear nothing, but] I hear everything. You wrote that the world doesn't need a savior, but every day I hear people crying out for one;" (3) afterwards, when the giant globe on the Daily Planet is loosened by an earthquake, Superman catches it, symbolically representing the burden of the world on his shoulders; (4) a short while later Superman lands on a Kryptonite-poisoned landmass, whereupon he is beaten, scourged, humiliated and finally stabbed in the manner of the impassioned Jesus; (5) after that, he is pushed into the water only to emerge, be revitalized by the Sun, and then return to destroy the landmass; and (6) finally, after heaving the landmass into space, Superman falls from the sky in a crucifixion position, flat-lines in a hospital on Earth, but in the end returns from the dead. Because of all this wonderfully executed Christian symbolism, this movie is without a doubt the greatest expression of Superman as Christ.

Nevertheless, it wasn't, as I said before, as if Singer was unaware of the other Christian symbolism that had developed around the Man of Steel since the time of *Superman II*. Consider three examples.

The first example is from *Kingdom Come*. In this mini-series, Superman, like Jesus, is depicted as departing the world of man—taking hope with him— only to return, in a "second coming," to restore justice and order. Indeed, in a later, connected story, the Man of Steel even asks the Reverend Norman McCay, "Couldn't you tell me how you see my journey fulfilling biblical prophecy? Could I be part of Revelation?"[35]

The second example is from *Superman: For Tomorrow*. In this mini-series, Superman's priest friend and pseudo-confessor, Father Leone, feels compelled to fall to one knee when the Man of Steel first appears to him, but is stopped from doing so by Superman himself, who says, "I don't think you want to do that." Later on, Father Leone is waiting for Superman by a lake, and when Superman finally arrives, Father Leone tells him that he kind of expected to see him, like Jesus, walking upon it. Finally, near the end of this story, Father Leone is transformed into the monster Pilate, appropriately named since he

---

news/featuresnews.php?id=4972 (accessed on February 19, 2010).
34   Bryan Singer, quoted in "4:11 with Bryan Singer" by Daniel Epstein, *Newsarama. com*, July 30, 2006, http://forum.newsarama.com/showthread.php?t=78755 (accessed on February 19, 2010).
35   *JSA: Kingdom Come Special; Superman* #1 (January 2009).

becomes unintentionally opposed to Superman the Christ-type.

The third example is from *Smallville*. In this TV series, Clark Kent is shown in a crucifix position in a cornfield,[36] and revealed, in a particularly powerful episode, to be everlasting.[37] In subsequent episodes, he would also be spoken of as a "savior,"[38] have his blood used to save countless people,[39] and would be pitted against Doomsday, a biblically-named villain representing the final enemy.[40]

Of course, Doomsday was himself taken from an even earlier stage in Superman's history. In 1992, in an event that sold more than six million comics, DC had Superman die at the hands of the monster Doomsday. Reminiscent of Michelangelo's *Pietà*, Lois/Mary holds the dying Superman/Jesus in her arms and says of Doomsday/Death, "You stopped him. You saved us all!"[41] In keeping with the Gospels, which talks about countless antichrists arising in Jesus's absence, Superman's death makes room for a number of false supermans to claim his identity and commit all sorts of evil in his good name. However, empty coffin and all, Superman comes back to life in time to defeat the anti-Superman, Hank Henshaw, and restore hope to the world once again.

## CHRIST OR CHRIST-TYPE?

Nowadays the Man of Tomorrow has become such a Christ-type that *Superman* literature, movies and TV series regularly make allusions, both comical and serious, to Superman being a god. Thus, in *Lois & Clark: A Superman Novel* we read,

> The *cell phone* rang.
> "God." Lois got it out and unfolded it, hoping for Clark.[42]

Or again, in *The Essential Superman Encyclopedia*, the Man of Steel, in true God-like fashion, is even spoken of as a necessary being, "Superman's greatest significance was that he may well have been the one truly indispensable figure in all creation—which perhaps explains why, in all the myriad parallel dimensions, there was always some form of Superman."[43]

It's not surprising, then, that some people have confused Superman as a Christ-type with Superman as an idol, or even, in a strange twist, Superman

---

36 *Smallville* season 1, episode 1.
37 *Smallville* season 3, episode 12.
38 *Smallville* season 9, episode 11.
39 *Smallville* season 9, episode 3.
40 *Smallville* season 8, episode 18.
41 Roger Stern, *The Death and Life of Superman: A Novel* (New York: Bantam, 1993), 130.
42 C. J. Cherryh, *Lois & Clark: A Superman Novel* (Rocklin, CA: Prima, 1996), 23.
43 Greenberger and Pasko, *The Essential Superman Encyclopedia*, 399.

as an antichrist. Thus, when *Superman: The Movie* first came out, Richard Donner, the director, said that he received numerous threats—presumably from Christians—for making obvious connections between Superman and Jesus.[44] Such Christians perhaps meant well insofar as they wanted to prevent Superman from becoming a secular *replacement* for Christ—something that admittedly is a possibility;[45] however, it would be better to emphasize the way things were intended to be, namely, that the more Superman becomes like Christ, the more Christ is revealed: the copy, as Plato says, ought to point to its Original, rather than the copy becoming falsely mistaken for the Original.

And Superman himself agrees. While Gog says, "Worship me,"[46] and Lex Luthor asserts, "They will worship me as a god,"[47] Superman constantly denies his literal deity, breaking up cults dedicated to his worship,[48] wrestling with his own inner demons (in *Superman* #666, no less), and, in *Superman: Godfall*, by stating plainly to Lyla and the Kandorians: "I'm not God. . . . I'm just a man." When the Atom asks Superman (who died and rose again) what Heaven is like, Superman humbly asks, "What makes you think I went to Heaven?"[49] Indeed, Superman would even agree with Nietzsche that people shouldn't put blind faith in him since such weakens individual dignity and resolve (though Superman wouldn't have a problem with people trusting in him for good reason and, of course, for accepting help when they can't save themselves).[50] Perhaps the right balance between seeing Superman as a Christ-type that enables, rather than a god-tyrant that stifles, is in *Superman: Peace on Earth*, which powerfully depicts Superman side-by-side with the Christ the Redeemer statue in Rio de Janeiro while at the same time making it clear that Superman's mission is not to usurp Christ but to be a Christ-like inspiration to people; thus, he says of world hunger, "It's not my place to dictate policy for humankind. But perhaps the sight of me fighting hunger on a global scale would inspire others to take action in their own way."

---

44 *The Making of Superman: The Movie and Superman II* (USA Home Video, 1980).
45 John Lawrence sees Superman and other superheroes as "secular counterparts of religious leaders." John Lawrence, "The Mythology of Superman," in *You Will Believe: The Cinematic Saga of Superman* (Warner Bros., 2006). And Christopher Knowles believes that "superheroes have come to *fill* the role in our modern society that the gods and demigods provided to the ancients." Christopher Knowles, *Our Gods Wear Spandex: The Secret History of Comic Book Heroes* (San Francisco: Weiser Books, 2007), xv.
46 *JSA: Kingdom Come Special; The Kingdom* #1 (January 2009).
47 *Action Comics* vol. 1, #900 (June 2011).
48 *Superman/Batman: Worship*.
49 The Atom, however, counters Superman by saying, "Because if you didn't, the rest of us have no hope." *JLA: Heaven's Ladder*.
50 *Superman: The Last Family of Krypton* #3 (December 2010).

ABOVE: ON THE LEFT, THE ONLY SON AND THE LAST SON IN *SUPERMAN: PEACE ON EARTH*; AND ON THE RIGHT, SUPERMAN PREVENTS FATHER DANIEL LEONE FROM BOWING TO HIM—A MERE CHRIST-TYPE, AND NOT CHRIST HIMSELF—IN *SUPERMAN: FOR TOMORROW*.

## SEDUCTION OF THE INNOCENT?

In the 1950s, Fredric Wertham wrote *The Seduction of the Innocent: The Influence of Comic Books on Today's Youth*, which argues that comic books and superheroes are unhealthy and dangerous. In his own way, Nietzsche would agree, for since he thinks Judeo-Christian morality is toxic, and since comic books, in particular, *Superman* comics, are permeated with such, *Superman* comics would be toxic and dangerous as well. At best, the Man of Steel and his fans would be like Jesus, "a case of delayed . . . puberty."

But it was this attitude toward Judeo-Christian morality, along with biblical motifs and stories, that prompted a strong response from Jerry Siegel and Joe Shuster, who, it seems, intentionally set out to subvert Nietzsche's antichrist super-man, first by making Super-Man a villain, and then, second, by making him a Judeo-Christian hero of the first order. And this subversion continued over the decades to such a point that Superman has now become the greatest modern Christ-type and, though his mythical purity and moral perfection aren't always appreciated in our postmodern age;[51] nevertheless, Superman remains an inspiration to many. As we are told in *Superman: Grounded* vol. 2, "Superman is just as important as a symbol as he is a hero. . . . Superman is an inspirational figure. He shows us how to be better people

---

[51] In the '90s, when Superman was killed by Doomsday, Herbert London wrote the following in Superman's obituary: "Superman died, not because Hollywood created a lumbering and exhausted facsimile, but rather because the country doesn't admire superheroes." Herbert London, "The Death of Superman," *First Things* 31 (1993): 11. Cf. Lev Grossman et. al., "The Problem with Superman," *Time* 163 (2004): 70-72.

ourselves by being the best person he can be." And to this I would only add, amen.

# Imitating the Saints

# CHAPTER FOUR

## GREEN LANTERN: WILLPOWER, NOT WILL-TO-POWER

"Power tends to corrupt," writes Lord Acton, "and absolute power corrupts absolutely."[1] While many of us probably agree with the general sentiment of this saying, few of us who are superhero fans would go as far as Lord Acton. The reason for this is we have a slew of extremely powerful yet morally superior beings to prove our point.... Or do we?

Green Lantern, or rather, the Green Lanterns, make particularly good case studies in this regard. Of all the DC comic book characters, the Green Lanterns—too many to mention here—show a whole spectrum of reactions to the temptation of power. Some, it's true, appear unaffected by the siren call of power and use what they have been given with a reasonable degree of moral responsibility, while others, in fact, often the most powerful of the Green Lanterns, are corrupted by their desire for power or even by their desires in general.

Indeed, it's no accident that one of the founders of the Green Lantern Corps, a so-called Guardian of the Universe, says, "I was there billions of years ago when we first decreed that the ultimate cause of chaos was emotion."[2] In the belief that emotions and desires are the cause of disorder and lawlessness, the Guardians severed theirs and formed the galactic police force known as the Green Lantern Corps, whose source of power, the Green Element as present in numerous power rings, depends, ironically, entirely for its potency on the willpower of its users. That is, while the Guardians seem to blame emotions and desires for all the evils of the universe, their own taskforce depends completely on emotional strength—the power behind the will—in order to achieve their objectives. So how can we make sense of this mess of desires, lack of desires, and the subsequent corruption or moral purity of those with or without desires? More to the point, what is the correct understanding of the desire for power? Willpower might be good, but is the will-to-power—the Nietzschean idea that we should desire power in order to achieve our own selfish goals?[3]

---

1 John Emerich Edward Dalberg Acton, *Essays on Freedom and Power* (Boston: Beacon Press, 1949), 364.
2 *Green Lantern* vol. 4, #43 (September 2009).
3 For more on this, see chapter three of this book.

We could hardly ask for a more fitting guide to help us examine these questions than Plato, in particular, the Plato of the *Republic*, since not only are some of the characters in the Green Lantern universe inspired by Platonic characters, such as the Guardians, but also many of the moral problems and their trappings, including the Green Lanterns' desire for power *qua* their power rings, are clearly addressed, and perhaps indirectly influenced, by Plato, who deals with the temptation of power in another story about rings: the story of the Ring of Gyges.

Consequently, in this chapter, I will begin by examining Plato's approach to desire and power, especially insofar as they are discussed in the Ring of Gyges story, and then I will try to apply these findings both to the Guardians of the Universe and various Green Lanterns in order to evaluate their reactions to, and for, power.[4] Finally, I will conclude with some additional comments on how Plato might need to be qualified in order to make him fit within a Christian philosophical framework.

## "NOW SUPPOSE THERE WERE TWO SUCH RINGS..."

The first book of Plato's *Republic* begins with Socrates and a few friends and acquaintances discussing justice, the central theme of the book as a whole. Ever humble (even if ironically so), Socrates begins by asking his first interlocutor, the sophist Thrasymachus, what he thinks justice is. Thrasymachus boldly replies that justice is that which is to the advantage of the stronger party, meaning that justice is simply a façade that rulers put on in order to manipulate those below them.[5] Justice, in other words, is simply a tool or a means to an end and not something good and lovely in and of itself.

In the second book of the *Republic* a slightly more refined version of this justice-is-a-social-construct argument is forwarded by Socrates's friend Glaucon, who asks, "Is justice good in all circumstances or the appearance of justice in all circumstances?"[6] Needless to say, Glaucon agrees with the latter, maintaining that *if* people can act unjustly without experiencing any of its negative effects, such as punishment or social instability, everyone would do so since injustice is more beneficial than justice. That is, the only reason why people act justly is because they are afraid of the consequences of not doing so—not, again, because they actually think justice is good in and of itself. To illustrate his point, Glaucon tells the story of the Ring of Gyges:

---

4     For another take on the Ring of Gyges and superheroes, see Jeff Brenzel, "Why Are Superheroes Good? Comics and the Ring of Gyges," in *Superheroes and Philosophy*, ed. Tom Morris and Matt Morris (Chicago: Open Court, 2005).
5     Plato *Republic* 348d.
6     Ibid., 357a.

An ancestor of Gyges of Lydia, a shepherd by all accounts, was in the service of the Lydian ruler of the time, when a heavy rainstorm occurred and an earthquake cracked open the land to a certain extent, and a chasm appeared in the region where he was pasturing his flocks. He was fascinated by the sight, and went down into the chasm and saw there, among other artifacts, a bronze horse, which was hollow and had windows set in it; he stooped and looked in through the windows and saw a corpse inside, which seemed to be that of a giant. The corpse was naked, but had a golden ring on one finger; he took the ring off the finger and left. Now, the shepherds used to meet once a month to keep the king informed about his flocks, and our protagonist came to the meeting wearing the ring. He was sitting down among the others, and happened to twist the ring's bezel in the direction of his body, towards the inner part of his hand. When he did this, he became invisible to his neighbors, and to his astonishment they talked about him as if he'd left. While he was fiddling about with the ring again, he turned the bezel outwards and became visible. He thought about this and experimented to see if it was the ring which had this power; in this way he eventually found that turning the bezel inwards made him invisible and turning it outwards made him visible. As soon as he realized this, he arranged to be made one of the delegates to the king; once he was inside the palace, he seduced the king's wife and with her help assaulted and killed the king, and so took possession of the throne.[7]

After recounting this myth, Glaucon goes on to declare, "Now suppose there were two such rings—one worn by our just person, the other by the unjust person. There is no one, on this view, who has enough willpower to maintain his morality and find the strength of purpose to keep his hands off what doesn't belong to him."[8] In this respect, at least, Lord Acton would agree with Glaucon.

Socrates, however, doesn't. And through careful steps throughout the rest of the book and on into other works, he attempts to show that justice is something to be valued in and of itself, meaning, of course, that power, even the power of magical rings, will not corrupt the good man. Plato's argument for this, often told in the form of a myth or "likely story," is as follows.

Ultimate Reality—God, we may even say[9]—is the eternal world in which the perfection of all things exist: it's the source of Beauty, Rationality, Knowledge, Moral Goodness, Happiness and so on. In our previous lives (for Plato, unlike Christians, accepts reincarnation as almost certainly true)

---

7   Ibid., 359d-360b.
8   Ibid., 360b.
9   Ibid., 613a-b.

we were disembodied rational souls that enjoyed perfect happiness insofar as we could contemplate and enjoy the beatific vision of Ultimate Reality in all its rational, moral and aesthetic perfection. However, one day our souls, exercising imperfect control over our emotional faculties (he doesn't say how this could be), looked away, so to speak, from Ultimate Reality and hence fell far from it, deep into the physical world, until our souls were cloaked in matter, which caused in us a kind of trauma resulting in almost total forgetfulness of our original home and happiness.[10]

Yet not all was lost. Innate within our souls is some knowledge, which elicits subsequent rational desire, for the shining beauty of our true home and happiness. However, though we have some knowledge of our true home, complete knowledge of such and the subsequent knowledge of the way to return there has been obscured through the devastating effect of following our base desires and emotions rather than our rational desires informed by knowledge of true happiness. Consequently, the goal of this life is to pursue knowledge and wisdom—to become lovers (*philos*) of wisdom (*sophia*), *philosophers*—which in turn will afford us a better idea about true happiness and how we can regain such.[11]

And what the philosopher discovers is that because true Happiness is connected with perfect Rationality, which in turn is connected with Moral Goodness (all three being united in perfect Beauty), the happy person is he who acts wisely and thus justly. The idea, moreover, is that such a person first knows what is rational and good (through *noûs*), and then uses his desires (*thumos*) to fervently apply these.[12] *Desires, in other words, are not bad in and of themselves but are bad only insofar as they over-rule the moral dictates derived from reason.* Furthermore, because our happiness resides in rational contemplation of Ultimate Reality and its content, such as Moral Goodness, Moral Goodness (along with all other aspects of Ultimate Reality) is good in and of itself: simply to contemplate and enjoy Moral Goodness (and the rest of Ultimate Reality) constitutes our very happiness.

This, then, will keep men of power, such as Plato's guardians (the philosopher-kings, who Plato thought should govern society), morally uncorrupted and trustworthy. Indeed, the rational, moral person may—and in fact, ought to—pursue earthly power not, as with Nietzsche's will-to-power, because such power has any value in and of itself, but because such power can be used to implement rational, moral order, which is, of course, one of the moral imperatives that our reason teaches us.[13] So, even if the moral person

---

10   Plato *Phaedrus* 249-250.
11   Plato *Symposium* 204d.
12   Plato *Republic* 410e.
13   Ibid., 433a.

had the power of the Ring of Gyges, he wouldn't use it for evil (since his happiness resides in valuing morality for its own sake), and, indeed, he would almost certainly use such a ring for good.

## "WHO GUARDS THE GUARDIANS?"

In *Tales of the Green Lantern Corps* Annual vol. 1, #3, we're presented with a pertinent question: "Who watches the watchmen?"—a question echoing the Roman satirist Juvenal's more ancient query, "Who guards the guardians?"[14]

According to Plato, the answer to this question is simple: the guardians, being wiser and thus morally superior to everyone else, govern themselves in addition to governing everyone else. Nevertheless, Plato would be the first to admit that although the guardians, being wiser and morally superior to others, should rule, it doesn't follow that they're *morally perfect*. As limited beings, the guardians would still lack some knowledge and thus would be capable of making moral mistakes. Of course, it's important to keep in mind here that unlike Christians, Plato had no clear conception of the will: he simply couldn't imagine a wise person, who knows that justice is essential to achieving true happiness, intentionally choosing to do evil, thus harming his own soul.

So how does this all apply to the Guardians of the Universe? Are they the universal equivalent of Plato's guardians or philosopher-kings? The answer appears to be yes for the following reasons.

First, the Guardians are, in virtue of their enormous longevity (which began ten billion years ago), unquestionably among the *wisest* and most knowledgeable beings in the DC universe. Thus, in one issue, a Guardian says, "My brothers and I have lived our lives by rational decision,"[15] and in another issue the Guardians are even referred to as "omniscient"—though this is probably hyperbole.[16]

Second, because of their great wisdom, the Guardians are among the *most moral* beings in the universe, and this is evident in the fact that they have dedicated their lives to "promoting an orderly rational cosmos," largely by founding, and guiding, the Green Lantern Corps.[17] In fact, when a confused Hal Jordan criticizes the Guardians, saying that their "greatest mistake" is not realizing that "life . . . is subjective," he is actually complimenting them since wisdom teaches that particular circumstances can only be morally assessed when all the relevant *objective moral principles* are in place.[18]

---

14  Juvenal *Satires* 4.6.346-347.
15  *Green Lantern* vol. 2, #200 (May 1986).
16  *Trinity*.
17  *Green Lantern* vol. 3, #55 (August 1994).
18  *Green Lantern* vol. 3, #67 (October 1995).

Third, the Guardians are, despite being among the wisest and most moral beings in the universe, *still capable of moral mistakes*. Nevertheless, because they are among the wisest and most moral, any mistakes they make should be forgiven by less wise, less moral beings since such beings would only do an inferior job of ruling. For instance, the Guardians should be forgiven for neglecting their emotions (an error that, among other things, played a part in prompting Hal Jordan's killing spree[19]). Or again, they should be forgiven for the massacres committed by their renegade androids, the Manhunters.[20] Of course, insofar as certain Maltusians, the race of beings from which the Guardians *later* sprang, are *not* among the wisest and most moral beings in the universe, such as in the case of Krona, neither are they to be followed nor their mistakes overlooked.[21] And insofar as certain Guardians have *mental illnesses that make them go mad*, such as with the Guardian Scar, they should *no longer be considered* among the wisest beings in the universe and so their moral mistakes should again not be tolerated.[22]

Consequently, Plato's explanation for the abuse of power—that power will only corrupt a person insofar as he is *ignorant* (wisdom teaching us to be moral)—goes a long way in explaining both why the Guardians, among the wisest beings in the universe, do a lot of good for it and should be its rulers, and also how, from time to time, they can (though far less than the rest of us) make moral mistakes.

It follows, then, that if the Guardians are as Platonic as they appear to be, we should expect that when they assembled the Green Lantern Corps, they only selected those who they deemed, in their best but still imperfect judgment, to be wise and deeply moral beings since the more moral a person is, the more likely it is that he will be able to control his desires and hence his power ring. But is this what we see? Did the Guardians make wisdom and morality important traits in those whom they selected to be Green Lanterns?

## "NO EVIL SHALL ESCAPE MY SIGHT"

The first thing to note is that not all Green Lanterns were in fact chosen by the Guardians. Consider the case of Alan Scott, the first human Green Lantern.[23]

Scott assumed his alter ego when he discovered a literal green lantern, whose flame told him, "You, who are to have this power, must use it to end evil. . . . The power shall be yours if you have faith in yourself. Lose that faith and you lose the energetic power of the Green Lantern, for willpower is

---

19  *Green Lantern* vol. 3, #49 (February 1994).
20  *Green Lantern* vol. 2, #141 (June 1981).
21  *Green Lantern* vol. 2, #40 (October 1965).
22  *Green Lantern* vol. 4, #44 (September 2009).
23  The original Alan Scott, not the New 52 one.

the flame of the Green Lantern!"[24] As we can see here, Scott's lantern clearly has intelligence and does endorse the morality of the Guardians insofar as it exhorts him "to end evil." And the reason for this is that it was the Guardians themselves who had forged the lantern, which in turn was given to a Green Lantern named Yalan Gur, who had used its power on Earth.[25] However, the intelligence within the lantern was damaged on Earth and so the Guardians lost contact with it and its user. Moreover, and more to the point, through a series of *coincidences*, the lantern managed to end up in the hands of Scott. It follows, then, that Scott wasn't chosen by the Guardians, much less chosen for his wisdom and moral uprightness. Thus, it would have been understandable if Scott had been overwhelmed by the power of the ring, which, thankfully, he wasn't.

Yet apart from Scott, probably all the other Green Lanterns were, either directly or indirectly (via another Green Lantern), chosen by the Guardians. Consider the case of the second human Green Lantern, Hal Jordan.

Abin Sur, a dying Green Lantern who crash-landed on Earth, selected Jordan to be his replacement because Jordan possessed two qualities. First, he was "honest," meaning that he was morally upright. Second, he was "fearless," which is to say that he wasn't afraid of evil or danger: he had enough willpower—*thumos* or emotional strength—to enforce his moral convictions.[26] Moreover, both of these qualities—commitment to morality and determination to uphold it—are evident in Jordan's famous Green Lantern oath:

> In brightest day, in blackest night,
> *No evil shall escape my sight;*
> Let those who worship evil's might,
> Beware *my power* . . . Green Lantern's light!

Although wisdom isn't mentioned as a criterion for Jordan's selection, Plato believed that wisdom is implied in morality, for you can't act morally without wisdom. Hence, on this account, we could say that Jordan was chosen because he was wise, in addition to being moral and determined. His soul demonstrated a proper Platonic ordering, reason ruling the desires and indeed reason using the desires to enforce its moral dictates. Jordan, in other words, would have initially passed Plato's Ring of Gyges test.

Of course, this doesn't mean that Jordan, or any of the Green Lanterns selected for their moral uprightness, can't make moral mistakes: if extremely wise and moral beings like the Guardians can err, how much more so can their subordinates. Nevertheless, some might argue that the enormity of the

---

24  *All-American Comics* vol. 1, #16 (July 1940).
25  *Green Lantern* vol. 3, #19 (December 1991).
26  *Showcase* vol. 1, #22 (September/October 1959).

mistakes Jordan made, not to mention those made by Yalan Gur and Sinestro, is evidence that, *contra* Plato, ignorance isn't enough to explain why these Green Lanterns, apparently chosen for their wisdom and morality, gave in to their desire for power and committed the evil they did. Thus, the question is: *are* there Green Lanterns who were in fact *chosen for their wisdom and morality* and who do in fact give in to their desire for power through something other than *ignorance*? In order to answer this question, I will examine the three most problematic cases in this regard: those of Yalan Gur, Sinestro and Hal Jordan.

## "REPENTED"

Yalan Gur was an extremely powerful Green Lantern assigned by the Guardians to protect Sector 2814 (the Earth's sector). In the distant past, he was nearly killed by a yellow beast—yellow being the color that makes the power of the green lantern ineffectual. Having the ability to remove the green lantern's weakness to yellow (which isn't the case in later comics), the Guardians removed it from Gur's lantern, thus granting him almost unlimited power. Overwhelmed by this, Gur soon became a dictator, ruling his sector from his base in ancient China. However, seeing that Gur couldn't handle unlimited power, the Guardians added a new weakness to his lantern—a weakness to wood. Consequently, Gur was mortally wounded by the wooden weapons of some angry Chinese peasants and, filled with "remorse . . . and guilt," didn't bother to heal his wounds and so died, his life-force being absorbed into his lantern and merging with the mysterious Starheart.[27]

So what do we make of this story? Does it constitute a challenge to Plato's theory of desire and power? Probably not. Gur was almost certainly chosen by the Guardians, and so would likely have been chosen for his wisdom and morality; however, when Gur received new power, he was forced to deal with new possibilities of being in the world—possibilities that caused him initially to err insofar as he involved himself in local politics. Yet the key thing here is that when Gur was shown the error of his ways, he became filled with remorse and guilt and, over the centuries, "the soul of Yalan Gur," we are told, "made peace with itself. It had repented. And so it gained control of its power."[28]

## "YOU HAVE NEVER UNDERSTOOD US"

Although Yalan Gur was a hero-turned-villain-turned-hero, Sinestro, another extremely powerful, former Green Lantern, is a villain through and through. Indeed, in 2009, he was voted the fifteenth greatest comic book villain of all

---

27  *Green Lantern* vol. 3, #19 (December 1991).
28  Ibid.

time.²⁹ But despite Sinestro's desire for power, his case poses even less of a challenge to Plato's theory of desire and power than Gur's. Why?

Although the Guardians' initial "tests showed Sinestro to be a deserving one and absolutely without fear," they later admitted that they made a "mistake" insofar as they didn't scrutinize Sinestro's character as carefully as they should have: Sinestro, it turns out, didn't simply want the power ring to help the universe but rather wanted to use it to set himself up as the dictator of his home planet, Korugar.³⁰ Thus, one Guardian tells Sinestro pointblank, "you have never understood us,"³¹ meaning that Sinestro *never* had the wisdom and morality that it takes to be a Green Lantern. Consequently, it's no surprise that he, like Gyges, was corrupted by "love of power."³²

## "NOT EVIL"

From earlier, we know that Hal Jordan was chosen by the Guardians for his moral integrity and willpower; in fact, he was the paradigm of what a Platonic Green Lantern looks like. Nevertheless, on at least two occasions, he made serious mistakes.

The first time he did so was when he resigned from the Green Lantern Corps because he wanted to spend more time with the love of his life, Carol Ferris. Although the romantically-inclined might find this understandable, Plato wouldn't have since according to him true happiness comes from being moral, and morality teaches us about our duties and proper prioritizing. Indeed, the only reason guardians—and here we could substitute Green Lanterns—become guardians in the first place is because they realize that they have a moral duty to lead others: if they neglect this moral duty, they can't achieve true happiness. Thus, by valuing his personal life more than his greater moral duties as a Green Lantern, Jordan acted unwisely. Nevertheless, this error, brought on by ignorance of the proper value of things, was later rectified by Jordan when the Earth was under attack. With new understanding that the planet is more important than his personal life, Jordan saw that he "can't sit idly by" and watch it be destroyed and so asked for "a chance to do what is right."³³ The Guardians agreed to restore Jordan's power but, testing to see if he was truly wise and moral, required that he play second fiddle to Guy Gardner, the fourth human Green Lantern. Jordan, realizing that doing what is right (following reason) is more important than his own pride (following desire),

---

29  "The Top 100 Comic Book Villains of All Time," *IGN: Entertainment Games.* http://comics.ign.com/top-100-villains/15.html (accessed on October 5, 2009).
30  *Green Lantern* vol. 2, #7 (July/August 1961).
31  *Green Lantern* vol. 2, #200 (May 1986).
32  *Green Lantern* vol. 2, #7 (July/August 1961).
33  *Green Lantern* vol. 2, #197 (February 1986).

agreed.

The second time Jordan acted unwisely was after Mongul and the Cyborg Superman murdered the seven million inhabitants of Jordan's hometown, Coast City. Wandering through the crater that was once his hometown, Jordan dreamt about the "power to be God" so as to resurrect the city and its inhabitants.[34] Consequently, when the Guardians refused Jordan such power, he defied them and even killed his close friend Kilowog in order to acquire the energy of the Green Lantern Central Power Battery, with whose strength, Jordan believed, he could "set everything right."[35] What's important to note here is that once again Jordan acted out of ignorance of the proper value of things; as Alan Scott said of him, "Understand, Hal's not evil. . . . He believes he's acting for the right reasons;"[36] indeed, shortly after, Jordan came to see that he "made terrible mistakes,"[37] and so, in true heroic fashion, sacrificed his own life to save Earth.[38]

ABOVE: ON THE LEFT, HAL JORDAN GENUINELY REPENTS OF HIS SINS IN *DAY OF JUDGMENT*; AND ON THE RIGHT, HE IS REDEEMED IN *GREEN LANTERN: REBIRTH*.

Of course some might still think that ignorance isn't enough to explain all the acts that Jordan as Parallax committed (in particular, the events of *Zero Hour*). Yet these people should keep in mind that it wasn't always *Jordan* doing these terrible things: after absorbing the Central Power Battery, Jordan was possessed by the fear-entity, Parallax, who amplified Jordan's emotions, in particular, his fear, which in turn over-ruled the moral dictates of his reason. Thus, many of the evils Jordan-Parallax brought about should be seen as ones

---

34  *Green Lantern* vol. 3, #48 (January 1994).
35  *Green Lantern* vol. 3, #50 (March 1994).
36  *Green Lantern* vol. 3, #55 (September 1994).
37  *Green Lantern* vol. 3, #0 (October 1994).
38  *Final Night*.

committed by a mentally ill (and thus not necessarily evil) Jordan. Consequently, I don't think the mistakes made by Jordan pose a serious challenge to Plato's theory of desire and power.

## "TO END EVIL"

I began this chapter by explaining Plato's theory of desire and power, which, in a nutshell, argues that because happiness comes from enjoying (among other things) justice for its own sake, the person who understands this—the wise person—will thus be a just person, meaning, among other things, that he, unlike Gyges, won't be corrupted by the desire for power. But even so, the moral person *will* desire power, but will do so only insofar as he understands that it's his moral duty (and hence his happiness) to lead, by serving, others. Willpower is good, but the Nietzschean will-to-power is bad.

And this is what we see not only with the Guardians of the Universe, but also with their chosen taskforce, the Green Lantern Corps. Nevertheless, while the Guardians and Green Lanterns ought to rule and police the universe so as "to end evil," they shouldn't be seen as infallible or incapable of making moral mistakes: they aren't. Yet even so, all such mistakes *can be*—though perhaps aren't always *best*, especially given free will and original sin—explained as the result of an acceptable level of ignorance.

# Imitating the Saints

# CHAPTER FIVE

## THE AVENGERS: GOOD GODS

When Asgard, the home of the Norse gods, fell from the sky and landed in Oklahoma, one Christian pastor nearby began his Sunday sermon by asking, "Small-g gods? Big-G? Are the Asgardians 'gods'? And if they are, well, where does that leave my God?"[1]

Although I feel for this pastor and his disrupted equilibrium,[2] it's clear that in the Marvel universe, of which the Avengers and Thor are a part, God—capital "G"—exists. Dr. Strange learns about Him from the massive but not all-powerful cosmic being Eternity, who says, "I and my brother, Death, comprise all your reality! Neither he nor I am God, for God rules all realities!"[3] Thanos, even when he acquires the Heart of the Universe and bests the Living Tribunal (God's supreme angelic servant), is naggingly aware of the Supreme Deity weaving the Titan's mischief for some higher purpose: "Was this my moment of triumph," he asks himself, "or but a facet of another's grand plan?"[4] And finally, the Fantastic Four and Spider-Man—all of whom have been Avengers at one time or another[5]—personally meet Him: the Fantastic Four by entering Heaven itself,[6] and Spider-Man when God appears as a homeless stranger to comfort the weary Web-Slinger.[7]

So God exists . . . but how do we reconcile this with the plurality of beings in the Marvel universe, and, more particularly, with the diversity found in the Avengers—diversity that includes a god like Thor? Moreover, how

---

1  *The Mighty Thor* vol. 1, #1 (June 2011).
2  In *Thor: Heaven & Earth*, a Catholic priest also has a crisis of faith when he meets Thor. But though pluralism presents a challenge to this priest's faith, Thor is shown to be wiser. Not only does Thor acknowledge that he himself is a mere creature, but he also emphasizes the mystery that surrounds us all by quoting from 1 Corinthians 15:50-52!
3  *Dr. Strange* vol. 1, #13 (April 1976).
4  *Marvel Universe: The End* #6 (August 2003).
5  The Thing became an Avenger in *The West Coast Avengers* vol. 2, #9 (June 1986), Mister Fantastic and Invisible Woman in *The Avengers* vol. 1, #300 (February 1989), the Human Torch in *The West Coast Avengers* vol. 2, #50 (November 1989), and Spider-Man in *The Avengers* vol. 1, #329 (February 1991).
6  *Fantastic Four: Hereafter*.
7  *The Sensational Spider-Man* vol. 1, #40 (September 2007).

should we understand this in light of Exodus 20:3, which commands, "You shall have no other gods before me"? In this chapter, I will try to articulate how God stands in relation to the Marvel universe. Although this will start as an exercise in mythology and ontology (a defense, as we shall see, of the plurality of diverse beings), it will end with an ethical argument, namely, that though the Avengers are many and diverse, they are unified in their love of the Good, which, I will suggest, is actually a love for God seen through a glass darkly.

## AVENGERS DISASSEMBLED

In the Marvel great chain of being, God is at the top—He's the first tier being—and though He can be spoken of and to, He is of a different category than all other beings. He is the Creator; everything else is creation. It's telling that in three instances that God is depicted—one in *Dr. Strange*,[8] one in *The Fantastic Four*[9] and another, as the Fulcrum, in *The Eternals*[10]—He is depicted as either Stan Lee or Jack Kirby, the literal creators of the Marvel universe.

In addition to being the Creator, God "is all-powerful and all knowing. He is the very essence of what holds reality in its place."[11] As such, God "sets the stage" for the drama of creation to play out.[12] However, though God is clearly transcendent and of a different category than all other Marvel beings, He is also immanent, interested and invested in what goes on in the realities He creates: "The play is your lives," He tells the former Avengers the Thing, Invisible Woman, Mister Fantastic and the Human Torch, "Your adventures become our exploration."[13] Just as an author has intentions as he writes, so too does God have intentions—perfect intentions—in His creation; He tells Spider-Man, "We all have a purpose, Peter. We all have a role to play."[14] And if the nature of God still seems ambiguous, He is clearly meant to be likened to the Judeo-Christian God, possibly alluding to Jesus even when He tells the heroic but suffering Peter Parker, "And, you know, if it's any consolation, I've asked a lot more from people much closer to me than you."[15] Indeed, "His only weapon," the Watcher tells the Invisible Woman, "is love!"[16]

Below God in the Marvel great chain of being—and switching categories

---

8  See *Strange Tales* vol. 1, #157-163 (June-December 1967).
9  *Fantastic Four: Hereafter*.
10 *The Eternals* vol. 2, #9 (May 2009).
11 Ibid.
12 *Fantastic Four: Hereafter*.
13 Ibid.
14 *The Sensational Spider-Man* vol. 1, #40 (September 2007).
15 Ibid.
16 *The Fantastic Four* vol. 1, #72 (March 1968).

from Creator to creature—is the Living Tribunal. Although likely second to God in authority (and third to God in power, after the wielder of the Heart of the Universe), the Living Tribunal is a mysterious figure of the Ezekiel 1 sort: like the "Living Creatures" of Ezekiel 1:6, each of whom have four faces, the Living Tribunal has four faces (three and a "void"[17]), and like the Living Creatures, who adore God in His throne room, the Living Tribunal is "the representative of The-One-Who-Is-Above-All."[18] The Living Tribunal's "task is to sit in judgment of events on the far end of the cosmic scale,"[19] and each of his three visible faces represents a mode of his righteous judgment: necessity, equity and vengeance. Each face can be likened to an angel in the Bible who pours out judgment in the name of the Most High,[20] and it's perhaps not unimportant that the Living Tribunal's face of necessity paraphrases Jesus ("Do unto others as you would have others do unto you") when he tells the She-Hulk, "Necessity is the Cosmic mirror which reminds us to always judge others as we would have ourselves judged."[21]

Below the Living Tribunal in terms of might, though not in terms of order of creation, is the wearer of the Infinity Gauntlet. Though the Gauntlet is sometimes spoken of as "the Mantle of Supremacy"[22] and its wearer sometimes claims to be God in terms of power and knowledge,[23] the power of the Gauntlet is power only over one reality, not all realities. Indeed, the Living Tribunal (not to mention God) can nullify the Gauntlet's power at will, but rarely does so because it's an important piece in the free will drama of creation.[24]

Following God (the first tier being) and the Living Tribunal (the second tier being) are a group of primordials called the cosmic beings or astral deities of the universe. These include the Celestials, Lord Chaos and Master Order, the Stranger, the Watcher, Galactus, Love and Hate, Kronos, Eternity,[25] and, most recently, the Chaos King (it's not very clear how he differs from Lord

---

17  *Silver Surfer* vol. 3, #31 (December 1989).
18  *The Infinity War*. In this story, The-One-Who-Is-Above-All is another name for God, and should not be confused with the prime Celestial, The One Above All, who is a mere Celestial—a servant of the Fulcrum (God). See *Thor* vol. 1, #287 (September 1979).
19  *The Infinity War*.
20  Exodus 12, 2 Samuel 24:16, 1 Corinthians 10:10, Hebrews 11:28, and Revelation 9:11.
21  *She-Hulk* vol. 2, #12 (November 2006).
22  *The Infinity War*.
23  *The Infinity Gauntlet* and *The Infinity War*.
24  *The Infinity War*. The importance of free will in the story of creation cannot be underestimated. Even a lesser deity such as Thor says, "If we save you from yourselves every time you stumble and fall, ask yourself what you must inevitably become? Puppets." *Thor: Heaven & Earth*.
25  *The Infinity Gauntlet*.

Chaos).²⁶ Most of the cosmic beings are beyond, and in some measure, cause, the physical fluctuations of the Big Crunch (the collapse of the multiverses) and the subsequent Big Bang (the explosion of the multiverses into a plethora of dimensions, universes and worlds), yet none of these beings are absolutely indestructible or eternal in the strict sense of the word: all suffer defeat at one time or another.

Below the cosmic beings are the fourth tier beings, the elders of the universe, who include the Collector, the Grandmaster, Chthon, Gaea (Mother Earth), and possibly Death. If Death is in fact an elder and not a cosmic being (the new literature suggests this, but not the old²⁷), then one possible way to relate the elders to the cosmic beings is to take a page from Hesiod's *Theogony*, which suggests that there are four primordial gods (Chaos, Gaia, Tartarus and Eros), who in turn give birth to all other beings. Chaos, for example, gives birth to Nyx (Night), who in turn gives birth to Thanatos (Death).²⁸

I believe something like this is also true in the Marvel universe, for when the Avengers Hercules and Thor ask Eternity why he helps them fight Thanos and Death but won't help them fight the Chaos King, Eternity replies: "Thanos merely wanted to kill everything. The Chaos King is the Darkness and Chaos that existed before existence itself. He is an anti-god, the void against which I am defined. He and I walk hand in hand. If I fight him, I fight myself."²⁹ Of course, this only helps clarify to some extent the positions of the Chaos King (Chaos) and Love (Eros or the force that pulls things together³⁰), and not Gaea (Gaia), who is a primordial goddess in Greek mythology and merely an elder in the Marvel universe.³¹ Nevertheless, both Gaia (Greek mythology) and Gaea (the Marvel universe) spring out of Chaos: as an equal in the mythology or as a subordinate in the Marvel universe.

Furthermore, in Greek mythology Gaia is supposed to have given birth to Uranus, together with whom she gave birth to the titans or giants. The titan Kronos, Hesiod reports, is the father of the gods, the chief of whom is the Olympian Zeus.³² As with the relation between the cosmic beings and the

---

26  *Chaos War.*
27  In the old literature, Death is often depicted as Eternity's opposite, which would make him or her a cosmic being. However, during the Chaos War, the Chaos King is depicted as Eternity's true opposite and Death is a clear subordinate. See *Captain Marvel* vol. 1, #27 (July 1973) for the old and *Chaos War* for the new.
28  Hesiod *Theogony* 116, 123 and 759.
29  *Chaos War.*
30  Empedocles, *The Poem of Empedocles*, in *Selections from Early Greek Philosophy*, 4th edition, ed. Milton Nahm (New York: Appleton-Century-Crofts, 1964), 114.
31  To add to the confusion, Gaea and the other elders in the Marvel universe wield the Power *Primordial*.
32  Hesiod *Theogony* 137 and 412.

elders, the relation between the elders and the sky fathers can't be perfectly understood within the framework of Greek mythology and polytheism. For example, in the Marvel universe, Kronos is one of the cosmic beings (a superior being) but in Greek mythology is a titan (an inferior being—one below the four primordials though still above the gods).

Nevertheless, Greek mythology certainly has some explanatory power. In the mythology, Gaia, for instance, is the mother or grandmother of the gods, including the sky father, Zeus, and in the Marvel universe, Gaea is said to be the mother of all the sky fathers—not just Zeus, but also Osiris, Odin and others. She tells Hercules, "I was the first to form out of chaos. I birthed the gods themselves. I am the true fount of creation . . . the source of all that the gods can do and have done."[33] Additionally, insofar as the sky fathers Osiris and Odin are depicted in the Marvel universe as subordinate beings, this largely agrees with both Egyptian mythology (where Osiris appears to have been one of the children of Ra, who himself, though uncreated, sprang from the watery-void, Nun[34]) and Norse mythology (where Odin is the child of the giants, who are the product of the cow Audumla, who in turn is the offspring of the two primordial elements, Fire and Ice[35]).

Of course, all this talk about tiers of beings only explains some things such as longevity and parenthood. We who have been influenced by Greek philosophy and Judeo-Christian theology might rightly maintain that that which is oldest is that which is strongest, wisest and most indestructible—Plato believes this to be true of the Forms and Judeo-Christians of God—but for us to project this onto Greek and Norse polytheism would be anachronistic. In both of these cases (not to mention in the case of their root source, Mesopotamian mythology[36]), the late-coming sky fathers—Zeus and Odin—were able to defeat their respective fathers (the giants) and claim supremacy even while the primordials lingered in the background.

In the Marvel universe, too, lesser beings, such as Thanos (an Olympian god modified by the Celestials[37]), can wield the Infinity Gauntlet, which in turn can defeat Eternity, and Hercules the sky father is able to best the Chaos King. Thus, in respect to created things in the Marvel universe, order of existence is one thing that separates the cosmic beings, elders and sky fathers

---

33  *Chaos War.*
34  Cf. Douglas Brewer and Emily Teeter, *Egypt and the Egyptians*, 2nd edition (Cambridge: Cambridge University Press, 2007), 98.
35  *The Prose Edda* 2.4-6. Also see *The Poetic Edda* 1.3 and 1.18.
36  In Mesopotamian mythology the second tier god Ea kills his first tier father, the primordial Apsu, and Ea's son, the third tier god Marduk, slays the first tier primordial goddess, Tiamat, to become the king of the gods. *Enuma Elish* 1.4, 1.69 and 4.104.
37  *Thanos* vol. 1, #1 (December 2003).

even if not much else, absolutely-speaking, does.

We should expect, then, that when we turn to look at the differences between Avengers—for my purposes I'll discuss Thor, the Hulk, the Wasp and Black Widow—that differences between them will rarely be absolute differences. So what makes them somewhat varied? I begin with Thor.

Gaea gave birth to the sky father Odin, who is the supreme god of the Asgardians, and together (Gaea in the guise of Jord and Odin as himself) they begot Thor.[38] In all likelihood, Odin claims the title of sky father and the powers that go with that office because he was directly, without the aid of a lower father, birthed by Gaea, an elder, whereas Thor is a lower god (a sixth tier being we could say) because his blood was diluted by having a sky father for a parent and not just an elder.

Most of the gods, including Thor's Asgardians, live in dimensions different from that of human beings, although through greater knowledge and magical powers, they are able to intervene in the human dimension more easily than humans can in the gods': Thor can generate a portal between the Asgardian dimension and the Midgardian (earthly) dimension just by waving his hammer, whereas a mere super-human like the Hulk or a mere human like the Black Widow can't do so. Of course, the key phrase is "more easily" since a super-human and human *can* enter the divine realms or dimensions by "mere" human means such as the magic of Dr. Strange or the very advanced technology of Stark Enterprises.[39]

The gods' greater magical ability also seems to give them greater resistance to the magical attacks of beings relative to their own stature. For example, although Lord Nightmare, who is a being roughly on par with the gods, was able to take control of "those with mortal minds," a god such as Thor remained unaffected.[40] Of course, this greater magical ability should not be mistaken for greater knowledge since the ability to do something isn't the same as the ability to *explain* how one did it. For example, few would argue that, on the whole (a key phrase), a Henry Pym or Bruce Banner is smarter or more knowledgeable than a Thor or Hercules; indeed, whereas both Pym and Banner can explain how to manipulate extra-dimensional space (as Pym does with his Pym Particles and Banner does when he transforms into the massive Hulk), Thor, though he manipulates the dimensions every time he teleports, can't really explain how he does so.

As with their magical abilities, the gods' strength generally exceeds that of humans, even super-human ones. When Skaar, son of the Hulk, asks, "Gods? So what? We've fought every monster and demon," the She-Hulk

---

38  *Thor* vol. 1, #300 (October 1980).
39  *The Avengers: Earth's Mightiest Heroes* season 1, episode 24.
40  *Chaos War*.

quickly replies, "You don't understand. Gods are a bit different."[41] And indeed, they are. "Among mortals," Hera tells the Hulk, "you may be the strongest one there is but Father Zeus could vaporize you with a thought," and although Zeus doesn't do so, he does soundly defeat the Hulk, chaining him up like Prometheus for vultures to pick at him. In fact, even though Loki magically possesses the Hulk in order to turn him against Thor, saying, "Only you brought near defeat to the mighty Thor,"[42] Thor, and not the Hulk, can lift the magical hammer Mjolnir, and Thor, not the Hulk, emerges victorious: as the Wasp says of herself and fellow Avengers, "Thor, we already know you are the strongest."[43]

Of course as with most everything in this graded universe, these kinds of statements are general, not unqualified. Consider two things. First, strength is an unclear term. Does it mean mere physical might or does it include, even leaving magic aside, other non-physical abilities? Graviton's power over gravity, for instance, is sufficient to defeat Thor and so he rightly asks, "Do you think I would surrender because of your supposed godhood? Perhaps I too am a god."[44] Second, even if, for the most part, gods are physically stronger than mere super-humans (seventh tier beings, we could say), a single demi-god, such as Hercules, can be physically defeated by a group of lesser (super-human) beings, which is what happens when Mr. Hyde, Goliath and the Wrecking Crew beat him within an inch of his life.[45]

And this raises the important question of what it means to be an "immortal" anyway. In metaphysics, we typically say an *eternal* thing is that which is "outside" of time, having no beginning and no end; an *immortal* thing is that which has a beginning in time but no definite end; and a *mortal* thing is that which has a beginning and definite end in time. In the Marvel universe, only God is eternal, and because all other beings are creatures (that is, are created by God), all other beings are either mortal or immortal. Animals and plants, of course, are mortal since they cease to exist upon physical death, but humans, and all those above humans, continue to endure after their bodies perish. Thus, in this sense, humans, and those above humans, can be called immortal. However, this needs to be twice qualified. The Living Tribunal, the cosmic beings, the elders, the sky fathers and the gods are sometimes called immortal proper since their bodies don't succumb to disease or old age,[46] whereas humans are sometimes called mortal because their bodies do

---

41   *The Incredible Hulks* vol. 1, #622 (February 2011).
42   *Hulk vs. Thor*, directed by Sam Liu (Marvel Animation, 2009).
43   *The Avengers* vol. 1, #220 (June 1982).
44   *The Avengers* vol. 1, #159 (May 1977). Also see *The Avengers: Earth's Mightiest Heroes* season 1, episode 7.
45   *The Avengers* vol. 1, #274 (December 1986).
46   *The Avengers* vol. 1, #48-50 (January-March 1968).

die because of disease and old age. Nevertheless, there is also a sense that all beings, save for God, can be unmade. Indeed, in the Marvel universe, all lesser beings have experienced this with the exception of Thanos and Adam Warlock, and even these could easily be unmade by God if He so wished.[47] In this way, it would be proper to call the Living Tribunal, the cosmic beings, the elders, the sky fathers, the gods and the humans "conditionally immortal," meaning that though they can continue to exist after their bodies die, they can still be unmade by God if He so wishes. Hence, only animals and plants are mortal, and it is imprecise to use the term "immortal" as a synonym for "god" when strongly contrasted with humans.

Now the Hulk, the Wasp and Black Widow are all ontologically on lower levels than the god Thor, though this is mostly in respect to lineage and age and only to a lesser extent in respect to natural immunities and abilities. In the Marvel universe, all four were made by God via His servants Eternity[48] and Gaea and in this respect are equals, but human beings, we are told, were given the finishing touches by the sub-sub-sub-sub-creator Odin ("Some whisper that he made the first man"[49]), which, if true, would mean that while Thor, as the son of Odin, was *begotten* by Odin (who, I hasten to add, was of course himself ultimately created by God), the Hulk, the Wasp and Black Widow were, in a more strict sense, *created* (or touched up) by Odin.

But just as not all gods were created equal in respect to ontological status, power and so on (I don't say worth), so too is it with humans. The Celestials, we are also told, long ago arrived on Earth and experimented with the human ancestors (the ones Odin made?), producing, in addition to the super-powered Eternals and Deviants, humans with the mutant X-gene, which either endows these super-humans with powers upon birth (as in the case of the Ultimate Wasp) or gives them latent powers which need to be unlocked by such things as radiation (as in the case of the Hulk).[50]

Mutations often appear very random and so it's unusual, though not impossible, for two mutants to share the exact same powers. Accordingly, because the longevity formula that Black Widow drank likely would give *any* human great longevity (her very ordinary partner also drank the formula and also got increased longevity), she should not be seen as a mutant with latent powers needing to be awakened by the formula.[51] The same is true of

---

47 *Marvel Universe: The End* #6 (August 2003).
48 Eternity says, "I am Adam Qadmon, the archetypal man, and in my bosom grew mortals, each on their various worlds! At first they were only algae in their great mother seas ... simple souls ... but over the eons, I advanced them ... from one cell to two, to many ... to man!" *Dr. Strange* vol. 1, #13 (April 1976).
49 *Thor* vol. 2, #83 (October 2004).
50 *Thor* vol. 1, #287 (September 1979).
51 *Black Widow: Deadly Origin*.

the Earth-616 Wasp (the Wasp of the regular Avengers universe), who was not alone in drinking Pym Particles and developing the ability to manipulate extra-dimensional space.[52] These two are both human. The Ultimate Wasp, however, is born with mutant powers,[53] and the Hulk, as we know, was born with latent mutant powers. In terms of ontology, then, the Ultimate Wasp and the Hulk (despite seeing his mutation as a "disease"[54]) would likely be seventh tier beings (homo sapiens superiors), while the Earth-616 Wasp and Black Widow would be eighth tier beings (homo sapiens). In respect to knowledge, power and immortality, the same things that I have said about the cosmic beings, elders, sky fathers and gods could be said of super-humans and humans: generally the higher beings are stronger, more knowledgeable and longer living, but all of this is, again, generally speaking.

So how does one make sense of all these beings, including other gods, given the existence of one supreme God in the Marvel universe? Doesn't God—the Judeo-Christian God, who is clearly the model here—say, "You shall have no other gods before me"?

The term "god" (lower case "g") is used in the Bible to describe not only non-existent deities represented in statues (such as Dagon in 1 Samuel 5:4), but also rebellious angels (such as Satan) and even, importantly, *human beings*. Psalm 82:6 reads, "I said, 'you are gods;' you are all sons of the Most High"—a passage quoted and elaborated on in John 10:34, where Jesus says, "Has it not been written in your law, 'I said, you are gods'? If he called them 'gods,' to whom the word of God came (and Scripture cannot be broken), do you say of Him, whom the Father sanctified and sent into the world, 'You are blaspheming,' because I said, 'I am the Son of God'?" Of course, Jesus's admitting that humans are "gods" (that is, created rational souls, spirits or persons) shouldn't be taken to mean that Jesus Himself is only a "god" in this sense: Jesus isn't just a "god" (a human being) but is also "God" (hence, "I am the Way, the Truth and the Life.").

The point here is that the existence of other "gods" is perfectly compatible with Judeo-Christianity as it is with the Marvel universe. Indeed, we should expect that if God is the Creator (essentially, that is), then it's actually *probable* that He would create more than just humans and angels (two types of "gods"). To say the Bible doesn't mention rational beings other than angels and humans and therefore such beings don't exist is to commit the fallacy of the argument from silence: true, we don't know if other "gods" (created rational aliens of all sorts) exist or not, but given the existence of God, such are likely, and we

---

52  *Tales to Astonish* vol. 1, #55 (May 1964).
53  *The Ultimates: Super-Human*.
54  *The Avengers* vol. 3, #74 (January 2004).

should delight in this probability.⁵⁵ Nevertheless, while the diversity of the Marvel universe may give us a hint as to what Heaven is like, Heaven will not be made up of any and all. If God is the Good, then the ethics of His creatures matter, and this is what I want to explore next.

## AVENGERS, ASSEMBLE!

In the Marvel universe, as in our own, ontological status—that which generally goes hand in hand with order of creation, longevity, power, knowledge, etc.—is no measure of moral goodness. Our universe has Satan and the Marvel, Mephisto: both are extremely old, powerful beings that happen to be very bad.⁵⁶ But this isn't just true of the devils. When wearing the Infinity Gauntlet, Adam Warlock foolishly imagines that a proper supreme being must not permit "good and evil to cloud his judgment,"⁵⁷ and even his "good" aspect, the Goddess, is nothing of the sort, imagining that goodness is something that can be forced, rather than wooed.⁵⁸ Indeed, Galactus and the Celestials massacre millions in the worlds they destroy; the goddess Hera shows her immorality when she tells the Hulk, "An oath to a monster means nothing;"⁵⁹ and Eternity himself is at odds with God, the Supreme Being and the Supreme Good, when he tells Dr. Strange, "I am above such petty emotions as gratitude!"⁶⁰ Power and privilege rarely, it seems, translate into right actions.

---

55   In the Marvel universe, as in our own, some misguided Christians view such ontological diversity in a negative light. Consider three examples. First, in *The Avengers* vol. 1, #171 (May 1978), Thor walks through a Christian nunnery and begins to feel a bit "uncomfortable," finally explaining to his companion, "E'en my father, Mighty Odin, who is called all-powerful, doth lay no claim to supreme divinity . . . and yet, t'would seem that many mark my very existence as an affront to this edifice!" Second, in *The Avengers* vol. 3, #28 (May 2000), Lupe/Silverclaw, who is the daughter of the goddess Peliali, tells the Avengers that the Christian missionaries that raised her tried to make her disbelieve (rather than properly understand in light of greater revelation) all the old stories and ways and were "nervous about my powers, which they considered ungodly." And finally, in *House of M*, shortly after most mutants on Earth lost their powers, Reverend William Ryker foolishly says in respect to the remaining mutants, "[This has been] foretold in Scripture for years now, and now the cleansing has finally begun. The abomination of humanity that was 'mutantkind' is now seen to be what it always was . . . a disease of our own decadence and indulgences. God's will has been done, and now it is up to man to finish His work [that is, kill the remaining mutants]."
56   Satan himself also exists in the Marvel universe and is distinct from Mephisto. See *Wolverine Goes to Hell*.
57   *The Infinity War*.
58   *The Infinity Crusade*.
59   *The Incredible Hulks* vol. 1, #622 (February 2011).
60   *Dr. Strange* vol. 1, #13 (April 1976).

So how has evil come to be? Hints are sown throughout the Marvel universe—hints in keeping with a basic Judeo-Christian account. In *Fantastic Four: Hereafter*, God tells the Four that they are His "collaborators," saying, "You're no one's puppets. . . . Nobody can do your living for you," and in *The Sensational Spider-Man* vol. 1, #40, when Peter asks God why he has been given his powers, God replies by showing Peter the scores of people he has saved along the way, saying, "They are some of the point, Peter." God creates because He loves to create, to be sure, but He creates rational beings, spirits or persons ("gods" of all sorts) for communion with Him—for them to commune with the Good—and to spread Goodness to others: "'Love the LORD your God with all your heart and with all your soul and with all your strength and with all your mind,'" Jesus tells us, "and 'love your neighbour as yourself.'"[61] Because good and evil only have meaning insofar as a person is free, God has given all His "gods" free will to choose between Good or evil, God or anything else that comes above God the Good: the true meaning, then, of "You shall have no other gods before me" is not to deny the existence of other gods, but rather to love everything properly, God and His Goodness above all else. Evil creatures, then, are simply those who value or elevate anything else above God the Good and His moral laws. The wise understand this, thus the Watcher tells the Dreaming Celestial, "The pulse that seemed to be completely random at first, but now registers with every cycle? That is what humans call a conscience. It's what recognizes and differentiates good from evil. It took me even longer to realize that the best thing to do was simply heed it."[62]

Though diverse and not particularly powerful in the grand scheme of things, the Avengers—here I'll limit myself to Thor, the Hulk, the Wasp and Black Widow again—also understand this.

To begin with, the god proper. Thor understands that the difference between right and wrong is important and so he tells "the slayer of the gods," Devak, "I have long agreed that some gods are malevolent and dangerous. But your inability to discern between good and evil makes you equally as dangerous."[63] And though "not exactly humble"[64] and at times brash ("Dropping a nuke on a problem isn't the Avengers' way, Thor."[65]), the God of Thunder loves the good. He can't abide Kang the Conqueror attacking the Wasp and others who are weaker ("Villain wouldst thou strike at women and babes?"[66]); he "spit[s] upon [the] unholy judgement" of the cosmic Celestials;[67]

---

61  Luke 10:27.
62  *The Eternals* vol. 2, #9 (May 2009).
63  *Thor* vol. 2, #78 (July 2004).
64  *The Avengers* vol. 1, #220 (June 1982).
65  *The Avengers* vol. 3, #63 (March 2003).
66  *The Avengers* vol. 2, #2 (January 1997).
67  *Thor* vol. 1, #300 (October 1980).

he is hospitable to a fault ("A stranger in need of the Avengers' help," he says as he opens the door to the villain Wonder Man[68]); he sides with the right even when it costs him personally (he abandons his 9th century Viking followers after several of them butcher innocents in a Christian monastery[69]); and he fights "in the name of justice,"[70] pledging, "those who practice evil shall be cast down beneath our heels!"[71] However, more than this, he, as a true hero, understands that justice is perfected or completed by love: indeed, by agape or sacrificial love, the supreme love, the love which the Bible claims is one of God's names.[72] Thor, as a lover of the good, loves justice (treating each as it ought to be treated) and mercy (going beyond, in a positive way, the commands of justice), saying, "I shall not falter in my resolve to protect this planet and save its people!"[73]

The Hulk, Black Widow and the Wasp are also dedicated to the good.

The Silver Surfer knows that "Bruce Banner," the Hulk's human side, "would die to give others life."[74] And the Hulk himself, though certainly not without flaws,[75] feels the same way when it comes down to it—here, saving Thor from the Collector ("He fought to free me from the Elder's control," Thor says, "No matter how he is attacked . . . the Hulk remains a hero"[76]) and there, sacrificing himself to Zeus to spare his family ("Here you are asking for miracles, offering yourself as a sacrifice," Hera mocks him, "Dying for other people's sins"[77]).

Natasha Romanova, the first Black Widow, is also flawed—she is deeply cynical[78] and has killed more than her share—yet she comes around to become a lover of what's right: "You have to see you're being manipulated," she tells Yelena Belova (the second Black Widow), "You have to do the right thing;" "I agree," she tells Daredevil, "Hunting down the Punisher is the right thing to do;" "I've decided," she informs the Winter Solider, "working with you to

---

68 *The Avengers* vol. 2, #7 (June 1997).
69 *The Marvel Encyclopedia*, 2nd edition (New York: DK, 2009), 336.
70 *Thor* vol. 1, #388 (February 1988).
71 *Thor* vol. 1, #300 (October 1980).
72 1 John 4:8.
73 *Thor* vol. 1, #388 (February 1988). Also see the 2011 live-action *Thor* movie, where Thor, as a Christ-type tells Loki, "These people are innocent. Taking their lives will gain you nothing. So take mine and end this." And then, dying, we hear the words, "It is over," echoing the words of the dying, sacrificial Jesus, "It is finished" (John 19:30).
74 *The Avengers* vol. 2, #12 (October 1997).
75 The events of *World War Hulk* and certainly *Hulk: The End* make this clear.
76 *Marvel Universe Avengers: Earth's Mightiest Heroes* vol. 1.
77 *The Incredible Hulks* vol. 1, #622 (February 2011).
78 *The Avengers* vol. 1, #351 (August 1992).

## Christian Philosophy and Superhero Mythology

honor Captain America's memory. . . . It's the right thing to do;" and to her long-time colleague Ivan, she states plainly, "You say I pick sides. I pick good guys. I pick kindness and mercy."[79]

Finally the Wasp, because of her lesser abilities, is often afraid. Yet precisely because of this, she is perhaps the most impressive hero of all, for she never fails to help those in need despite the great danger to herself. Thus, Captain America solemnly states, "[She is] the bravest person I know,"[80] and Henry Pym does likewise, saying, "Janet van Dyne was the very essence of heroism, of duty. . . . All over the world, she was a symbol of selfless humanity."[81]

Every one of these heroes—all of the Avengers, I would dare to generalize—love the Good, and since the Good is an aspect, or essential property, of God, they can be said to love God either clearly or through a glass darkly.

ABOVE: ON THE LEFT, THE AVENGERS—LOVERS OF THE GOOD—IN *THE AVENGERS: EARTH'S MIGHTIEST HEROES*; AND ON THE RIGHT, THOR DISCUSSES FAITH WITH A CATHOLIC PRIEST IN *THOR: HEAVEN & EARTH*.

## GOOD GODS

In one particular *Avengers* comic, Duane Freeman, the representative of the American government to the Avengers, tries to pressure Iron Man into accepting more minorities into the team, to which Iron Man replies, "We don't recruit for skin color. The Avengers aren't about equal representation—the squads are too small for that. We're about getting the job done—and that's it. We've had minority members for years—from black and Hispanic heroes to gypsies and mythological gods. We'd never exclude anyone—anyone—

---

79 *Black Widow: Deadly Origin*.
80 *Marvel Universe Avengers: Earth's Mightiest Heroes* vol. 1.
81 *The Avengers* vol. 3, #20 (September 1999).

because of their race."[82]

And something similar is true of God, both in the Marvel universe and our own. The Creator is pleased to accept not only human beings, but also any and all free willed creatures—"gods"—He has made; yet He accepts them under one condition: they must love Him . . . they must, that is, love the Good.[83] In this way, the Avengers are a model for us all, for though they are diverse, they are unified: unified in their love of Goodness Himself.

---

82  *The Avengers* vol. 3, #27 (April 2000).
83  The most important aspect of loving God is confessing one's sins or injustices so that reconciliation can take place. Of course, in the Marvel universe this particular activity isn't depicted a lot; however, we could well imagine it happening since none of the Avengers are beyond saying their sorry when they have done something wrong as the post-*Siege* events have shown.

# CHAPTER SIX

## THE HULK: IDENTITY AND "GOD'S BOUNDARIES"

"We live in an upside down world," remarks director Ang Lee, "biblically, we lost Paradise."[1] This comment, I believe, is central to Lee's vision for his 2003 movie *Hulk*, based on the Marvel comic book series *The Incredible Hulk*. In past films, Lee demonstrated an array of philosophical approaches, but in this movie, the philosophical themes and concepts are religious ones, especially Judeo-Christian ones. For example, when Bruce Banner (a.k.a. the Hulk) blows up a frog during a lab test, his long-time love, Betty Ross, jokes that now they know who they can turn to when a "plague [of] frogs start falling from the sky." The allusion to the ten biblical plagues is clear, as is the implication that Bruce is a kind of Moses figure who, on the side of the spiritual and the age-old normative, will be a future hero. Further allusions to, not to mention direct statements about, Bruce being like the biblical Isaac and being "predestined" to a certain life path are woven throughout, yet all of these are in service to the general theme of losing paradise.

What is "paradise" in this movie such that it can be lost? Probably drawing on the general ethos of Taoist and Mahayana Buddhist sympathies with the natural world, but fleshing these out in more Judeo-Christian terms, Lee seems to suggest that "paradise" is the state of peace or harmony that exists when the laws of nature are discerned and respected. The heroes are those who obey objective natural laws, especially those pertaining to what is natural to humanity, and the villains are those who, in the words of Banner's father, David, desire the "power to go beyond God's boundaries!" In the movie, Lee makes it clear that the villains are the metaphysical materialists, who reduce human nature and personal identity to mere bundles of matter and then treat them accordingly, while the heroes are those who recognize that human nature is an immaterial essence and treat it as such. In strict metaphysical terms, the vision of human nature and natural laws in *Hulk* is also at odds with most Chinese conceptions of human nature and natural laws, but this, I believe is accidental to Lee's purpose in the film. What I shall argue, then, is that *Hulk* can be seen as a polemic against materialistic reductionism of human nature and ethics,

---

[1] Ang Lee, "Commentary on *Hulk*," in *Hulk*, disc 1, directed by Ang Lee (Universal, 2003).

and that this polemic takes place vis-à-vis the preferred vision of human nature and natural ethics which is, very roughly, Judeo-Christian.² Lee, of course, isn't himself a Jew or Christian, but Stan Lee, the creator of the Hulk is Jewish with Christian sympathies, and it makes sense that insofar as Lee wanted to stay true to Stan the Man's vision, that these conceptions of human nature and ethics would be apparent in the film.³ Is Bruce Banner identical to the Hulk? If so, how? Can genetic engineering affect human nature? How does ethical behavior shape personal identity? Is all genetic modification of human nature unnatural? These questions, and other ethical ones having to do with human nature in *Hulk*, will be explored throughout.⁴

## MATERIALIST MONSTERS

*Hulk* begins with David Banner,⁵ Bruce Banner's father, working in his military lab on an experiment having to do with genetic improvement. We read notes like "Regeneration is immortality," which is highly suggestive that David is a metaphysical materialist, who believes that man is nothing but a bundle of matter or a collection of accidental properties. We infer this since if David believed that a human being is a rational soul, spirit or person, which is an indivisible substance with essential properties (an essence), then he would very likely believe that human beings possess a kind of immortality already (one independent of bodily existence), and hence wouldn't likely be so obsessed with genetic immortality.

But besides likely being a metaphysical materialist obsessed with bodily immortality, David is also—not coincidentally, the movie seems to suggest—a bad man. When the military properly forbids him to experiment on human subjects, he defies them and experiments on himself. In addition to the immorality of disobeying a direct order for no good reason, David is a bad

---

2  Judeo-Christian conceptions of human nature and ethics, of course, owe a great deal to Greek philosophy, in particular, Aristotle, who was the first to speak philosophically about substances, properties, accidents and essences.

3  Lee apparently loves Western superhero comics, especially Stan Lee's Marvel heroes. Thus, even in *The Ice Storm*, Stan Lee's *Fantastic Four* plays an important metaphorical role in the film, and in *Hulk* Ang Lee says plainly, "I'm a translator of that comic world." Ang Lee, "The Unique Style of Editing Hulk," in *Hulk*, disc 2, directed by Ang Lee (Universal, 2003). In the Marvel universe, the chain of being starts with a Judeo-Christian-like God, followed by a host of lesser entities, including the Living Tribunal, the cosmic beings, the elders, the sky fathers, the lower gods, and so on. See chapter five of this book for more details.

4  For more on Hulk and personal identity, see Kevin Kinghorn, "Questions of Identity: Is the Hulk the Same Person as Bruce Banner?" in *Superheroes and Philosophy*, ed. Tom Morris and Matt Morris (Chicago: Open Court, 2004).

5  In the comic books it's Brian Banner, not David Banner.

man because he fails, after having injected himself with an experimental drug, to take precautions to prevent his wife, Edith, from getting pregnant, ultimately resulting in her conceiving a child with altered DNA (I take it that, all things being equal, it's immoral, and not "genetic discrimination," for a person intentionally to try to conceive when the risk of the child having a serious birth defect is high). Furthermore, when the military discovers that David experimented on himself, they shut him down, and in a fit of rage (take note), he kills Edith while trying to dispose of his experiment, his son, Bruce.

Later on, when David is finally released from prison, he kidnaps Betty Ross, Bruce's girlfriend, and expresses his extreme annoyance that she wants to "cure [Bruce], fix him." To David the materialist, social Darwinism, the ethics endorsing "survival of the fittest," is most logical. Thus, he sees the powerful but out-of-control Hulk to be the true person, and Bruce to be "a weak little speck of human trash." In his Hulk state—internally, a state of foggy rationality—Bruce actually agrees, calling his normal state "a puny human." That David agrees with the fairly dull-witted Hulk is important since both largely act sub-human rather than super-human, all the while imagining it the other way around. Thus, Ang Lee tellingly admits, "Sometimes I think the father is the real Hulk." That is, the materialist is the monster.

David's argument, then, assumes, in true materialistic fashion, that there is no natural, proper, essential or "designed" pattern for how things—the world around him and his own person—should be, and so there is really no reason for him not to do as he pleases. And since what pleases him is to experiment on himself and his child, there is no reason for him not to do so; thus, he says, "It's the only path to the truth that give men the power to go beyond God's boundaries!" David obviously doesn't believe in a literal God, but rather uses God as a metaphor for the notion of indivisible essences and the proper functioning of such. Moreover, since unchanging wholes and the proper functioning of such wholes have a normative or ethical dimension which forbids man from doing *whatever* he likes, David rails against this ethical dimension as well, speaking with admiration for "a hero of the kind that walked the Earth long before the pale religions of civilization infected humanity's soul!" Savage, amoral "heroes" of the social Darwinist kind is what David the metaphysical materialist clamours for.

But David isn't the only metaphysical materialist monster in the movie. Major Glenn Talbot, a former solider now working in the private sector, is the other materialist in the movie and, not coincidentally again, is also the secondary villain. Talbot has a keen interest in the genetic experiments that Bruce and Betty are working on, but while Bruce and Betty want to use their experiments to find cures to benefit humanity, Talbot wants to privatize their research and use it for military purposes, ultimately, to make money. This is the first suggestion that he is a villain. Later on he becomes clearly so when he's not opposed to murdering Bruce in order to get his sample of the Hulk DNA: "I'm going to carve off a piece of the real you," he says. Talbot's social Darwinian ethics ("I'm stronger, so I can take what I like") suggests he's a metaphysical materialist since he appears willing to reduce Bruce/Hulk to his DNA (a part of his physical makeup), rather than seeing him as a rational soul, spirit or indivisible essence with inherent personhood and inherent rights. Bruce/Hulk is matter to be exploited.

## SOUL AND BODY

Against the metaphysical materialists are those who respect "God's boundaries" of stable essences and natural laws. Bruce and Betty are the foremost proponents.

We know that Bruce was born with an altered genetic code that boosts his immune system. Thus, when his experiment with gamma-infused nanomeds (nanobots that help repair the body from the inside) goes wrong, he (risking his life to save his assistant's) miraculously survives. However, the experiment-gone-wrong further alters his bio-chemistry. Does Bruce's altered DNA mean that he is no longer himself?

To begin with, it's the metaphysical materialists—the villains in Lee's movie—who imagine that one's personal identity is one's DNA (on account of DNA being bio-chemistry, which is, in turn, matter). Against them the movie makes it clear that if a person were identical to his DNA, then any alternation to his DNA would imply the literal loss of self, which is implausible and certainly not true of our hero, Bruce.

To elaborate, consider gene therapy. If we were to fix any broken genes in our bodies, we would, in fact, be curing not the same person, but creating a new one. The therapy wouldn't save "me," but would in fact kill "me" and create a new man. Moreover, imagine that in the course of this treatment "I" suffered traumatic brain damage such that "I" lost many or most of my memories. If "I" am identical to my memories *qua* bio-chemistry (organized by my DNA), then in losing memories, "I" would, again, literally cease to be "me." The improbability of this is expressed in our ordinary language, "I forgot something" *not* "I died." As we shall see, when Bruce's DNA is radically altered (not once, but twice), he is still clearly shown to be himself.

True to the spirit of the early comics,[6] Ang Lee makes it no secret that although Bruce's body has undergone an alteration, it's still *his* body and *he* is still *himself*. But what holds the unity of the body together through change, and what constitutes Bruce's personal identity? The answer to both of these

---

6   In *The Incredible Hulk* vol. 1, #3 (1962), we are told that the Hulk "isn't really just an inhuman monster to be destroyed. . . . He's Bruce Banner!"

questions is the human soul or spirit as roughly conceived of by Judeo-Christianity.

When Bruce becomes the Hulk, Betty, who knows Bruce "better than anyone," immediately recognizes the green monster to be Bruce vis-à-vis his eyes or "the window to the soul." Or again, when Bruce-as-the-Hulk later goes on a rampage, Betty tries to calm him down and this conversation ensues:

> Bruce: "You found me."
> Betty: "You weren't hard to find."
> Bruce: "Yes, I was."

Betty could see, where others could not, the truth of the matter, namely, as she later explicitly states, that Bruce-as-the-Hulk is "a human being." She can recognize the indivisible soul or spirit inside the green monster, and we, the audience, were meant to see this as well. In his director commentary, Lee says his obsession with CGI in the movie (including being the principle actor in the Hulk motion capture suit!) wasn't so much to make a spectacular smash-fest, but rather was "to unify" that which was previously separated. This is to say that while in the comic books and TV shows the Hulk always looks radically different than Bruce, in *Hulk*, Lee intentionally tries to let Bruce's soul or spirit shine through the green body by mapping Eric Bana's eyes and facial features onto the CGI Hulk: "The challenge was could I make Bruce Banner and the Hulk one person, instead of like in the comics or TV series where there are two actors or two different entities."[7]

By showing the unity of Bruce through CGI, Lee makes an important metaphysical statement about the nature of the soul or spirit, arguing, consistent with the general Judeo-Christian theme throughout, that the human soul or spirit is best conceived of as a substance with both essential and accidental properties.

Central to this is the notion that some essential properties in the human substance are non-degreed, meaning they are either 100% present or 100% not. The essential property "having the ultimate capacity for rationality," "having the ultimate capacity for language," and so on are such properties and if these properties aren't present, the substance isn't a human substance or soul.

Of course, based on the behavior of Bruce-as-the-Hulk, it might not seem as though the Hulk has all of these; indeed, he himself even spoke of "that mindless Hulk," and certainly, if taken literally, being mindless would disqualify the Hulk from being human. However, this language is rhetorical,

---

7  Ang Lee, "Evolution of the Hulk," in *Hulk*, disc 2, directed by Ang Lee (Universal, 2003). In addition, we are told that Lee was chosen to direct the movie because what comes through in all his films is "the humanity," and here, the humanity of the Hulk.

rather than metaphysical, and, more importantly, this confusion stems from a misunderstanding between ultimate capacities and lower capacities.

The human person—in our case, Bruce—is a soul or spirit. This means, among other things, he can still be himself or a human person without a body (the ancient Chinese just as much as Jews and Christians talk about the possibility of such "disembodied ghosts"). Because Bruce's Hulk body, brain and bio-chemistry are different than his human body, brain and bio-chemistry, Bruce—as a soul—can't (or at least not optimally) demonstrate his ultimate capacity for rationality, language and free will in his Hulk body. His Hulk body, in other words, doesn't have the lower capacity that Bruce's human body does for rationality, language and free will. Nevertheless, the absence or near absence of demonstrable, empirical evidence of these ultimate capacities doesn't at all mean that such ultimate capacities are absent. All it means is that the lower capacity—or bodily capacity—isn't there.

To clarify, take a baby in the mother's womb, an infant, a mentally handicapped person or one who is brain-dead. If we have reason to believe that the soul or spirit is that which animates the body (I will discuss this shortly), then the beating heart of a baby in the mother's womb makes it extremely likely that a human soul or spirit is present. However, the baby in the mother's womb can't demonstrate its ultimate capacity for rationality, language and so on because its lower capacities aren't developed yet; nevertheless, insofar as it's a human soul, it must necessarily possess these ultimate capacities in a non-degreed way. If we think the baby is ensouled, then it is 100% human, not 40% or even 99%. Ditto for the infant who can't demonstrate much or any rationality early on, the mentally handicapped person and the brain-dead. The same reason that Talbot is immoral for wanting to kill the Hulk (it's not a human person) is the same reason it's immoral, all things being equal, to engage in abortion, infanticide and eugenics.

Now in the course of this, I've assumed that the soul doesn't merely have a body in the same way that a captain "has" a ship. Christianity (and the ancient Chinese religion in its own way) has long insisted that the soul's connection to the body is more intimate than this, and this intimacy is what Lee tries to demonstrate through the soul-in-the-body CGI depiction of Bruce-in-the-Hulk. The general idea is this: the soul is prior to the body, to be sure, but it also gives rise to, and guides, the development of the body via the body's DNA. The ultimate capacity for the soul to develop or form a body with both general human features (arms, legs, etc.) and also specific ones (facial features, fingerprints, etc.) means that it's likely that even if the material the soul has to work with has been altered, the body's form will likely still both be humanoid and demonstrate unique features determined by the particular soul's "this-ness" or the essential property that differentiates one human soul from another. This is why Christianity depicts our new bodies in Heaven as ones still *visibly* similar to our current ones, why the Hebrews (and Chinese) tend to depict human ghosts as observably similar to their embodied forms, and why the Hulk is both humanoid and has Bruce's facial features.

In terms of controlling the formed body, the soul and its faculties direct the brain, which in turn controls the actions of the body. The soul affects the body, but, crucially, the body also affects the soul. When DNA is altered, bio-chemistry changes, including the bio-chemistry in the brain (scientists have only recently discovered that our actions literally alter our brains). The result is that the soul can no longer move the body as it previously could, but must now move it in accordance with the new biological makeup (its different lower capacities). The body and soul are intimately related (as Jews, Christians and the ancient Chinese insist), but not, as with the materialists, reducible to each other.

## THE HULK EVENT

So what exactly *is* "the Hulk"? Lee has called *Hulk* a "psycho-drama,"[8] which suggests that it's primarily about the *psuche* or soul and its faculties, such as the conscious mind, the subconscious mind, free will, memory and emotions. "The Hulk," of course, can refer to the large, green skinned body that Bruce takes on, but in terms of psychology and metaphysics, it's best thought of as an "event," such as a flash of lightning, the dropping of a ball, or an explosion of anger.

When Betty first encounters Bruce-as-the-Hulk she hypothesizes that Bruce's "anger is triggering the nanomeds," which in turn change Bruce's human body into the Hulk. In other words, the Hulk is an event triggered by rage. But this is still just Hulk 101, and Lee would take us further.

Discussing his movie *Crouching Tiger, Hidden Dragon*, Lee says that "crouching tigers" and "hidden dragons" have to do with what lies below the surface, in particular the hidden "passions, emotions, desires—the dragons hidden inside all of us."[9] In his commentary on *Hulk*, Lee says that a common theme in all of his movies, and especially *Hulk*, is that of repression or what the human spirit holds back or "hides;" to say that we have "dragons hidden inside all of us" is, in more particular terms, a way of saying "we all have a Hulk inside us."[10]

---

8  Ang Lee, "The Incredible Ang Lee," in *Hulk*, disc 2, directed by Ang Lee (Universal, 2003).
9  Ang Lee, et al., *Crouching Tiger, Hidden Dragon: A Portrait of the Ang Lee Film Including the Complete Screenplay* (New York: Newmarket, 2001), 76.
10  Lee, "Commentary on *Hulk*." This idea is also very true to the comic books, where in a dream-like sequence the Hulk tells Bruce, "The Hulk is your own dark

The Hulk event, then, is an event triggered by anger, but not only anger flowing from conscious understanding (which we will return to), but also from subconscious—repressed—thoughts and memories, which Lee especially identifies with "anxiety" and "fear" (and in Bruce's case, the anxiety of having watched his father murder his mother). Thus, it's not accidental that our first glimpse of the Hulk is while Bruce is dreaming (an uncontrollable, often fear-inducing event), and that the Hulk is also first introduced to the external world by stepping from the shadows (often associated with fear of the unknown) into the light. Bruce describes the Hulk event as "being born or coming up for air" or as "a vivid dream . . . [of] rage, power and freedom," to which he adds, "And you know what scares me the most? When it happens, when it comes over me, when I totally lose control . . . I like it."

Bruce likes losing control vis-à-vis irrational fear, not because he knows that this is proper, right or good, but rather because he likes the numbing feeling that rage brings about. Strong hate often overcomes strong fear.

But this is the perverse, subconscious Hulk event (known, in the comics, as "the Devil Hulk"[11]). The hate, anger or rage that drowns out the anxiety brought on by repressed memories is no long-term or healthy solution to the problem. What is repressed must be brought to light and dealt with or else all sorts of disorders, including multiple personality disorders, can result; unexercised ghosts hinder the natural harmony of the soul, body and external world and so mustn't be allowed to manifest in irrational spurts of anger.[12] Unbridled power is what David Banner dreams of, but he is, we recall, the villain.

If fifty years of the Hulk has taught us one thing, it's that the solution isn't to label all anger bad, but rather to recognize that anger is good in and of itself, and must be naturally or properly manifested, which is to say manifested in the service of rational deliberation aimed at truth. This no easy task for human beings, much less one with the Hulk's bio-chemistry; however, it can be done.[13] For example, when the three genetically altered dogs attack Betty,

---

thoughts, your own anger, your rage!" *The Incredible Hulk* vol. 2, #315 (1986).
11   Tom DeFalco and Matthew Manning, *Hulk: The Incredible Guide* (Toronto: DK, 2008), 129.
12   In *The Incredible Hulk* vol. 2, #377 (1990), we are told that Bruce suffers from a multiple personality disorder, but in this very issue, his personality is unified through the work of the psychiatrist to the superheroes, Dr. Samson.
13   For the first two hundred and seventy issues of *The Incredible Hulk*, Bruce-as-the-Hulk couldn't rationally cause himself to become the Hulk, even though as the Hulk he did have enough rational control to occasionally do heroic deeds; however, in *The Incredible Hulk* vol. 2, #272 (June 1982), Bruce was able to improve on this to the point where he could even rationally cause his transformation into the Hulk. Needless to say, this is the ideal way to control anger. However, when new writers took over *The*

Bruce-as-the-Hulk knows that he has a moral duty to protect the weak and, with this rational, moral consideration in mind, summons his anger to fuel his body to proper action, namely, to defend the weak. He does this again when he prevents the F-22 from crashing into a crowd of people on the Golden Gate Bridge. These acts are the demonstration of the human essential property "to have the ultimate capacity to act morally," and so we can say that by acting morally and heroically, Bruce-as-the-Hulk flourishes in his humanity. The Hulk body might be harder to control than the human body and so moral praise and blame will be a bit different;[14] however, the way they need to be controlled is the same, namely, with the higher faculties in the soul controlling the lower ones.

## A PARABLE ABOUT PARADISE

I've said that Bruce and Betty are those who respect "God's boundaries" of stable essences and natural laws, while metaphysical materialists like David Banner and Glenn Talbot are those who don't. I've argued that Bruce and Betty correctly understand human nature to be a substance with a number of essential properties and that giving these properties full consideration, and acting in accordance with them (in particular, the ultimate capacity for morality) is natural and right. It's natural and right to consider the Hulk a person and treat him as such, and its unnatural and immoral not to; it's natural and right for Bruce to try and protect Betty from the dogs (especially since he himself was in no danger of dying), and it would be unnatural or immoral if he hadn't. The materialists are the real monsters in *Hulk* since they have an unnatural conception of human nature and, based on this unnatural conception, treat humans unnaturally.

What I've assumed throughout, however, is that part of what's natural to humans is to have the ultimate capacity not just for rational thought in general, but scientific thought in particular. It's natural for humans to want to study the physical world, and it's natural, all things being equal, for them to want to test, experiment and discover. Our heroes, Bruce and Betty, understand this well.

Nevertheless, as with most aspects of life, there are tremendous complexities involved in this. For example, gene therapy, which has to do with restoring a broken original state, seems natural enough, but is it also natural to experiment with genes that aren't obviously broken? Even if we have some conception of what is natural to the human body, do we understand this perfectly? Could our bodies, at one time in the past—in Eden—have been like the Hulk's in that they could grow larger and heal faster? Is our current

---

*Incredible Hulk*, this was undone to some extent.
14  "I should have known that Bruce Banner isn't always responsible for what the Hulk says and does," says Bruce's pal Rick Jones. *The Incredible Hulk* vol. 1, #6 (1963).

"normal" really natural or is it still somewhat unnatural? What are the precise limits of human nature and the human body, such that if crossed, they would no longer be themselves?

Lee's proposal in *Hulk* is that "we lost Paradise" by defying "God's boundaries" of real wholes and stable natural laws, which, while not always obvious to us (hence the aforementioned questions), nevertheless need to be sought out as best we can. If we don't do this, we will be like Adam and Eve, who rebelled against God's natural laws, or the metaphysical materialists in *Hulk*, who manipulate human nature in ways that are unnatural and unjust, seeing Bruce as an animal to be experimented on, not a human person, a soul, with inherent rights, dignity and worth beyond any animal.

# CHAPTER SEVEN

## Spider-Man: Power and Responsibility

*Spider-Man* has twice been adapted into Japanese manga, and both times the results have largely disappointed western audiences upon their translation into English. Why this disappointment? There are many potential reasons, but arguably the most significant is that the background story explaining why Peter Parker chose to become Spider-Man—that is, the realization that Uncle Ben's death could have been prevented if he, Peter, had acted more responsibly with his spider-powers—is completely omitted in the Japanese manga. This points, by counter-example, to an important reason why *Spider-Man* as a comic book succeeds and *Spider-Man* as a manga fails: the presence of a clearly indicated *moral* reason for Peter's transformation.

The manga Spider-Man is marked by a moral relativism nurtured by the metaphysics of Shintō-Buddhism, and so he's presented merely as a powerful masked man who lives a carefree and largely directionless life. Depth and moral gravitas are nearly nonexistent. On the other hand, the Spider-Man of Western comics, and even more so, the recent Hollywood movies, finds his grounding in the ethics of the Christian tradition, which provides both the necessary boundaries in which real moral problems can present themselves, and the means by which such problems can be resolved. Indeed, nothing is more central to understanding both Peter's transformation into Spider-Man, and the subsequent internal struggles that result from this choice, than the influence of Uncle Ben, who, paraphrasing Jesus's "to whom much has been given, much is required,"[1] famously tells Peter, "with great power comes great responsibility."[2] Consequently, what the failure of the manga version brings to our attention is that Spider-Man stripped of his Christian ethics is no longer Spider-Man at all.

I'm not concerned here to make the case that Spider-Man is a Christian per se, though I think a good case could be made; rather, I want to explore the ethics that define Spider-Man, and these are, broadly speaking, Christian in character. Central to this examination will be the elucidation of the Christian understanding of freedom and justice, both of which are intimately connected with what in philosophy is usually addressed under the topic of the problem

---

1  Luke 12:48.
2  *Amazing Fantasy* vol. 1, #15.

of evil. This problem has taken different forms, but I will focus on its typical formulation in terms of the following: given the real and significant effects of evil, how can an omnipotent (all-powerful), omniscient (all-knowing), and perfectly good God exist? As we shall see, this philosophical problem is of considerable interest to Peter Parker.[3]

## "I HAVE CALLED YOU FRIENDS"

God, so the Christian tradition maintains, is the totality of all perfections. He isn't merely powerful; He is the perfection of Power. He isn't simply loving; He is the perfection of Love. He doesn't just exist; He is the Ever-Existing One. He isn't rational; He is the perfection of Reason itself.

Nevertheless, there are many things that God can't do, and yet these many things may be summed up in a single principle: *God can't do the logically impossible*. That is, God can't act against His own nature; He can't change who He is. Since God is the one absolutely perfect being, He has no lack, which implies, amongst other things, that He can't change His attributes—He can't go from perfection to imperfection. And because God is perfected Reason or Logos—that is, the totality or source of all rationality—He can't do anything irrational: He can't make 1 + 1 = 3 or override the Law of Contradiction. So, let me repeat it: God can't act against His very nature.

Yet if God lacks nothing, why did He create people in the first place? That is, for what purpose were humans made? Since God is the Creator, He acts in accordance with who He is: He loves to create, and so He brings into existence many things, such as the billions of galaxies billions of light years away, simply for His delight. Moreover, since God is Love itself, He deeply values friendship—one of the great forms of love.

But what does friendship entail? Friendship is only meaningful if it's *free*; love requires rational choice. It's a logical contradiction to say that God can *force* creatures to love Him *freely*: He can't do that, for He can't do the logically impossible. So, God created humans (and possibly other rational creatures as well) because He loves to create, but also, and far more to the point, *He made them to be friends with Him*: one of the important revelations of the New Testament is that Jesus says to those who love Him, "I have called you friends."[4] People might not change what God is, but their free choice to be friends with Him is something that God can't bring about by His own power, and so the human choice to love God freely is something of inestimable worth

---

3 For more on the relation between responsibility, power and superheroes, see Christopher Robichaud, "With Great Power Comes Great Responsibility: On the Moral Duties of the Super-Powerful and Super-Heroic," in *Superheroes and Philosophy*, ed. Tom Morris and Matt Morris (Chicago: Open Court, 2004).
4 John 15:14-15.

# Christian Philosophy and Superhero Mythology

to the Creator.

In this way, prayer, one of the key ways humans can express their friendship with God, isn't some magical process that automatically causes certain things to come about: prayer is praising the Divine Friend for being such a good friend; it's asking the Divine Friend for help when one needs it; it's questioning—sometimes angrily, though never disrespectfully—the Divine Friend why such and such things happen; it's a mode of communicating with another, albeit a far greater, free being. Prayer takes God, and friendship with God, seriously. And this we see not only with many famous biblical heroes, such as Abraham, David and others, but also with Peter Parker, for instance, in *The Amazing Spider-Man* vol. 2, #33 (Peter questions God about 9/11), vol. 2, #46 (Doctor Strange recommends Peter pray for guidance), and Annual #21 (Peter thanks God for the blessing of a good wife).

ABOVE: PETER THANKS GOD FOR HIS WIFE, MARY JANE, IN *THE AMAZING SPIDER-MAN* ANNUAL #21.

## "CAN'T YOU RESPECT ME ENOUGH...?"

So according to Christian ethics, God gave people free will to be friends with Him, which, since God is also the perfection of Happiness and Love, also means that God made people for infinite Happiness and Joy. Nevertheless, people have to *want* these things; they have to *choose* them. "Can't you," Mary Jane asks Peter in *Spider-Man 2*, "respect me enough to let me make my own decisions?" Peter, much like God Himself, of course, says yes.

Yet here is the catch. Unlike Peter, God is also perfect Holiness and perfect Justice. He can't change who He is, and so if people want to be friends with Him and if they want to be happy, then they must be holy and just. No evil, not the smallest speck, can be in the presence of the burning purity that is God. As the Ark of the Covenant demonstrates (quite visibly in *Raiders of the Lost Ark*), the impure can't see the face of the Holy God and live; God *can't*—it's a logical contradiction to say that He could—put aside His holiness, and it's also impossible for Him, because of His very nature, to ignore injustice.

Therefore, humans must use their rational minds to discern right and wrong—justice and injustice—and choose to do right if, quite literally, they want to be happy. But what is justice?

Justice means treating each as it ought to be treated, wherein the value of each depends on either God's creative choice (that is, the value God assigned to each thing or person He made) or God's own nature (where God's own value is a sheer fact or a given that He Himself can't alter). Thus, for instance, while it's just for a man to love himself, it's unjust to love himself the same as an ape since this entails loving a greater thing, a rational soul, on the same level as a lesser thing, a non-rational soul. Or again, and more to the point, while it's just for man to love himself and his opinions, it's unjust for him to love himself and his opinions to the same extent as, or more than, God and His justice, since God (the Uncreated Being) is of far greater value than a man (a created being). So while justice is absolute, the rightness or wrongness of a given act depends on knowing the value of each thing considered and then choosing to act accordingly. The failure to choose to act in accordance with justice is what is known as injustice, evil or sin.

Of course all of this is crucial to understanding both Jesus's maxim "to whom much has been given, much is required" and Uncle Ben's "with great power comes great responsibility." If a person has been given great power by God, then he is expected—if, for the moment, for no other reason than that the fulfillment of such an expectation is good for its own sake—to do great acts of goodness with that power; if the person has been given limited power, then God expects lesser things of him: the justness of a given act often varies according to what one is and has.

Some might complain and say, for instance, that God is unfair to make some people super-human and others not (given, of course, the Marvel universe and the existence of super-humans); but God doesn't act unjustly: while super-humans might enjoy *more* unique pleasures, which are good in and of themselves (such as great strength), super-humans are also expected to use their powers to benefit *more* people, or, if not more people, at least to benefit people in *more* extraordinary ways; thus, at the end of the movie *Spider-Man*, Peter rebuffs the offer of a romantic relationship with Mary Jane because, on top of his concern for her safety, he thinks that he can't both be with her and live up to the responsibility of his power: "This is my gift," he says, "This is my curse."

Consequently, it misses the point to think that being super-human is always better than being simply human: the point, according to Christian ethics, is that all people need to be just and act properly, which depends on what one is and has, and, if we are to follow Doctor Strange's advice and Peter's example, we should ask for God's help in doing so. Moral success is measured not by being the most powerful, but by doing what we should with what we are and have, like the woman in the Gospels who gave both of her coins—a meagre sum, but all she had—as opposed to the rich men who gave much larger amounts but a fraction of their wealth.[5] This is also why Dr. Otto Octavius is right when in *Spider-Man 2* he tells Peter, "Intelligence is a gift and you use it for the good of mankind." In Octavius's case, the misuse of his great intelligence ultimately leads to terrible consequences: theft, the murder of the medical professionals seeking to help him, the terrorization of countless citizens, and ultimately his own demise. It is only Peter's heartfelt appeal to Octavius to reclaim his formerly held principle that prevents further disaster.

So having great power isn't unqualifiedly better than having lesser power. Everything depends on what a person chooses to *do* with that power. Furthermore, as we see in Peter's relationship with Mary Jane and the poverty he suffers because of his refusal to either steal or seek financial boon for his services to the city, the choice to act justly can be extremely painful at times; as Aunt May, Peter's fount of moral wisdom and herself a Christian (as evidenced by her recital of the Lord's Prayer in *Spider-Man*), says in *Spider-Man 2*, "[Embracing the hero within means] sometimes we have to give up the thing we love the most . . . even our dreams." Nonetheless, the choice to do the right thing will, on top of being satisfying in and of itself, *ultimately* result in happiness for the individual.

Consider, for example, the first *Spider-Man* movie. By reneging on his promise to Uncle Ben to paint the kitchen and by failing to stop the criminal who robs the manager at the wrestling event, Peter is initially shown to act according to his own distorted or purely selfish desires instead of doing what he knows to be right. He is unjust because people ought to keep their promises (all things being equal), and if people have the power to stop a criminal, especially with little trouble, people also have a duty to do that. However, throughout the movie Peter becomes more and more just insofar as he chooses to focus on something greater than himself: justice and responsibility based on what he is and has been given. Thus, when Norman Osborne, in the guise of the Green Goblin, asks Peter why he bothers helping people, especially when they will eventually hate him for it, Peter replies simply, and yet profoundly, "Because it is right." Osborne ridicules this sentiment because he rejects the universal moral law, which the Christian tradition—the tradition that has shaped Peter's ethical outlook—has typically seen as flowing out God's very nature. Osborne sees morality as completely relative, claiming that the masses exist to lift "the few exceptional people on their shoulders." He is driven by dreams of "power" with which he can achieve his own selfish ends, meaning, of course, that he would have rejected the maxim "with great power comes great responsibility."

---

5   Mark 12:41-44.

Moreover, and to the point, it isn't a matter of Osborne choosing happiness, while Peter chooses duty. As I've said, acting justly and dutifully may require one to forgo certain pleasures at the moment, but, since God is the source of both justice and happiness, he who acts justly will ultimately be happy. Thus, in *The Amazing Spider-Man* vol. 1, #500 the spirit of Uncle Ben asks Peter simply, "Whatever it is you do now, whatever it is you've become, tell me, Peter, are you happy?" to which Peter, who has acted justly and dutifully, replies, "It's the damnedest thing, but . . . I am. I'm happy."

## "WE ALWAYS HAVE A CHOICE"

So what about the problem of evil? What can be said to those who insist that the presence of evil precludes the existence of an omnipotent, omniscient and perfectly good God? Let's follow the solution to this problem via Peter's own struggle with this dilemma, beginning with Peter's experience of the three key attributes of God which pertain to this problem: omnipotence, omniscience, and perfect goodness.

In *The Amazing Spider-Man* vol. 2, #49 Peter and Mary Jane have been living apart for some time, which is taking a serious toll on their relationship. No matter what they themselves try to do, it looks as if nothing can prevent their final separation. Indeed, in this issue we see Peter flying out to Los Angeles to meet up with Mary Jane at the exact same time as she flies out to New York to meet up with him: both desire to rebuild their marriage, but both, arriving in their respective cities, get the impression that the other isn't interested in such since neither are in their home cities. The issue initially reads like a tragedy—a vivid demonstration of man's limited knowledge and power in a daunting, uncaring universe. However, as both re-board their planes to head to their home cities, something beyond coincidence happens. A bolt of lightning strikes the plane that Peter is on, forcing it to land in Denver, where, remarkably, Mary Jane's stopover is. Peter and Mary Jane somehow manage to bump into each other in the airport and from there take the initial steps to reconciliation. Given what we already know of Peter's conversations with God, it ought to have been clear to Peter that there is a Being in the universe who not only *knows* the future (hence, this Being knows Peter's and Mary Jane's schedules and intentions) and has the *power* to use lightning to land an airplane and bring two individuals together at the exact same place at the exact same time, but also *cares* about Peter and Mary Jane—this Being doesn't want them to get divorced and where their best efforts to prevent this fail, He has the ability to step in and help out.

So that's God, but what about evil? In *Peter Parker, Spider-Man* vol. 2, #48 (appropriately entitled "The Big Question"), we see Peter explicitly asking God why He allows the people that Peter loves—good people—to suffer.

## CHRISTIAN PHILOSOPHY AND SUPERHERO MYTHOLOGY

Peter's question is particularized, but we can extend it to ask why God allows evil to befall anyone. What is interesting in this issue is that God, like God in the book of Job, appears to speak back to Peter, claiming that "this is all part of my grand design" and that Peter gets "to figure it out for [himself]," which will "make all the difference in the world." Is this just God evading the issue? Is this God playing with Peter, like a cat with a mouse? Or does this suggest that God doesn't really know the answer, and that there is no solution to the problem of evil?

The Christian ethicist would answer no to each of these questions. The solution to the problem of evil is implied in the very answer that God gives, namely that Peter gets "to figure it out for [himself]." Figuring out something requires not only a rational faculty capable of understanding but also the *free will* to choose between possible beliefs that arise as a result of such knowledge. Free will makes "all the difference in the world." God, as perfect Goodness, *wants* all people to be just and good but He can't *force* people to *choose* to be good; He can't, once again, do the logically impossible.

So what is evil such that its presence is compatible with the existence of an omniscient, omnipotent and perfectly good God? Strictly speaking, evil is simply the absence or privation of a good that should be present. Evil is choosing to value a lesser thing—oneself or one's opinions—over a greater thing (God and His justice). This means that God didn't create *evil*; God created *free will*, which is one of the greatest things imaginable, yet the very goodness of this thing lies precisely in its *potential* to do one thing or another—to love a greater thing over a lesser thing (justice) or vice versa (injustice, evil, sin).

Of course some might say that this is a valid solution to the problem of *moral or chosen evil*, but what about so-called *natural evil*, such as diseases, earthquakes and so on?[6] While neither the *Spider-Man* comics nor the movies address this type of evil, there are at least three possible solutions to this type of evil, at least two of which flow from the concept of moral or chosen evil and so are intimately connected with Peter's own struggle.

The first solution begins with the claim that human beings aren't the only types of free creatures that God made—that perhaps, among other things, He made angels, who are invisible and extremely powerful. As free creatures, these beings would, like humans, have the ability to choose to be just or unjust. Typically the Christian tradition has maintained that some such beings chose their own way over God's, and so became evil or "fallen." And, because angels were originally closer to God than men were, their punishment was greater than ours, as is consistent with "with great power comes great responsibility."

---

6    In other chapters in this book, I talk about two kinds of badness: moral badness (which I call evil proper) and non-moral badness (which includes every other type of badness, including aesthetic badness, physical badness, etc.).

The result is that these fallen angels or demons exist within God's creation and, because God respects their free will just as He respects ours (or else freedom wouldn't matter in the first place), they have some freedom to unleash evil in the world; for instance, they can cause diseases, tidal waves and so on. In this way, natural evil isn't natural at all: it's simply moral evil *qua* demonic activity.[7]

The second solution, which may be taken as an alternative to or in conjunction with the first, is that following on the principle of justice that states that the higher is responsible to rule the lower and the lower is dependent on the higher, when Adam, who God made the ruler of the planet, rebelled against God (Adam's *superior*), God, acting justly, cursed Adam in kind insofar as all that was *inferior* to Adam and those connected with him would henceforth be in rebellion against him and his own: man's emotions will rebel against his reason, animals will attack humans, and the entire natural world will turn on people through storms, through biological malfunction (physical deformities, diseases and death), and so on. In this way, all people suffer for the sin of their superior (Adam), and while it would be unjust if this suffering made people evil (it doesn't, though people might have a greater disposition to do evil, which is known as "original sin"), there is no reason to think it unjust that people, *qua* descendants of Adam, feel the effects of his choice. So once again, natural evil isn't natural at all if by natural we mean "the way God intended it." As before, natural evil is intimately connected with free choice and moral evil.

The third solution to natural evil, which, once again, may be taken on its own or with both or either of the previous solutions, states that when God made people, He made them separate from Himself. Yet people can't exist in a vacuum; they have to be *somewhere*—in some plane or field of existence wherein action and interaction can take place. This plane or field is known as the physical world, which acts according to physical laws. But inherent in the very goodness of the physical world is its potential for harm: the same tree that provides people with food can topple over and crush them; the same fire that gives humans light can burn them. God could, of course, intervene and prevent many of these evils (miracles are logically possible after all), but if He were to do so every time, it would render the whole purpose of physical laws obsolete, thereby implying that such were not a good creation.

## DEALING WITH VENOM

According to Christian ethics, then, evil exists precisely because God is good. That is, God's creative goodness is what motivates Him to create free willed people in the first place, and it's His moral goodness that motivates Him to

---

7   Alvin Plantinga, *God, Freedom, and Evil* (Grand Rapids, MI: Eerdmans, 1996), 55-59.

respect these people enough to let them choose to do evil. God, so the Gospels maintain, loves people enough to let them lock themselves in Hell, which should be understood as the willed separation from He-Who-Is-The-Source-Of-All-Happiness-And-Existence; in simpler terms, Hell is the shadowy place on the very fringes of non-being where the only thing that exists is the soul and its choices—nothing more.

Yet if this is the case and if, as I said, no evil, not the smallest speck, can be in the presence of the burning purity that is the perfectly righteous or just God, then how can God, who can't act against His own nature, *logically* allow any who have sinned to be in Heaven? How can anyone who has chosen to imbibe the fatal drink of injustice be rescued?

The Christian solution to this ethical problem, which is very much connected with *Spider-Man 3*, is *mercy*. According to the law of justice, if someone sins against you, he must repay you in order for the debt to be no more. If he can't repay, then the blemish or scar of injustice remains. Since human beings have committed sin against God, they must repay Him in order for their sins to be removed. But the problem is that no human can repay God completely, and so humanity's only hope to be holy again—its only hope to be happy again—is for God to show it mercy, which is a form of agape or sacrificial love. Yet because God is Justice itself, He can't simply wave His hand and make injustice disappear; His very nature prevents Him from dismissing injustice as if it weren't there. So God Himself has to pay the price; He has to pay the human debt of sin. And God, so Christian ethics maintain, did this very thing through His Son, Jesus.

As the "Son of Man"[8]—that is, as a man, but also as the eldest and first born of creation[9]—Jesus is properly able to represent all men just as Adam once did (thus, Jesus is called "the New Adam"[10]); and as the "Son of God,"[11] Jesus is able, among other things, to live the morally perfect life. As a result of this latter point, death can't hold Him since death represents the separation of man from God which was brought about by man choosing injustice (that is, by choosing injustice, man also chose death or separation from True Life, God). Because death can't bind Jesus, He is able to rebuild the bridge between man and God, and because Jesus, representing all people, paid the price of human injustice, He is also able, as the Debt-Payer and Ultimate Superhero, to offer mercy to all who acknowledge Him as their true representative. That is, by being perfectly *just*, Jesus is able to give *mercy* to all who ask for it. However, because Jesus loves justice and mercy, He also expects people to love these as

---

8   Luke 19:10.
9   Colossians 1:15.
10  Romans 5:12-21.
11  John 5:25.

well. The Christian, in other words, must be one who, mirroring Jesus, shows a proper love and understanding of mercy. And this, as I said, is what we see Peter doing in *Spider-Man 3*.

The movie begins with Flint Marko (a.k.a. the Sandman) fleeing from the police after accidentally killing Uncle Ben in an attempted carjacking. Marko's line throughout is "I'm not a bad person; I just had bad luck." Of course, according to the law of justice, Marko is a bad person not only for attempting to steal another's car but also for carrying around a loaded gun which, accidentally or otherwise, ended up being used to kill an innocent man. Marko may not be as bad as people think, but he is still bad.

Meanwhile, a symbiotic alien entity known as Venom lands on Earth and attaches itself to Spider-Man's costume. This alien has the property of amplifying the emotions of its host, in particular, the aggressive ones. Consequently, when Peter finds out that Marko is responsible for the death of Uncle Ben, Peter's anger exceeds the limits of justice and becomes its perversion: revenge. Revenge isn't the noble sentiment of justice, which demands each thing be treated as it ought to be and that, failing just treatment, some debt for injustice must be repaid. No; revenge not only wants to repay in kind, but also wants to keep on attacking, keep on hating. For instance, justice demands that if a person steals my comic book, he return the book and compensate me for any other suffering I have been inflicted with as a result of this act; however, revenge not only wants the book back and proper compensation given, but also expresses a hatred for the perpetrator and yearns to see him suffer.[12]

Near the end of the movie, Spider-Man gets the better of Marko and is thus faced with a choice: will he take revenge—thus signifying his own degeneration from the principle of justice "with great power comes great responsibility"—or will he show mercy, thus revealing his moral growth through the perfection of this principle. Of course, being a man who largely reflects Christian ethics, Spider-Man does as we expect him to, saying to Marko, "I forgive you."

## "IT'S THE CHOICES THAT MAKE US WHO WE ARE"

At the heart of Christian ethics lies a particular recognition about the nature of God as the perfection of all things, and a particular perspective on the free will of rational creatures. The solution to the problem of evil is provided in terms of these two principles. Rational creatures are given the choice to act in accordance with, or against, justice; that is, rational creatures are given the tremendous blessing of freedom, though this blessing can quickly become a

---

12 Revenge says with the distraught Spider-Man, who just witnessed the Green Goblin murder his girlfriend, Gwen Stacey, "Only one man's going to die this day—and, mister, it won't be me." *The Amazing Spider-Man* vol. 1, #122 (July 1973).

self-made curse since such creatures can choose to accept, or reject, a life lived according to the divine principle "with great power comes great responsibility." Spider-Man chooses to live up to this principle—most perfectly so at the end of *Spider-Man 3*, where he offers forgiveness to a man most of us more imperfect creatures would hate.

# Imitating the Saints

# INDEX

aesthetic 2, 4-5, 9n, 11, 62, 80, 119n
agape (sacrificial love) 18, 22-23, 27, 36, 64, 68, 100, 121
allegory 2-3, 8, 12
Alpha Flight (characters) 31n, 58-59
American 4, 17-19, 25-31, 53n, 59n, 63, 70, 83, 101
angel 6, 14, 16, 39-41, 44, 47, 55, 57, 66, 89, 91, 97, 119-120
antihero 21n, 26
Aquinas, Thomas 2n, 42, 61
Aristotle 32-33, 104n
art 2, 4-5, 12
the Avengers (characters) 19, 45, 89-90, 92-102
*The Avengers* (comic books and movies) 21n, 50, 89n, 98n

Ba'al 6, 10
Batgirl (character) 13, 44, 48, 50, 52-53, 52n
Batman (character) 13-14, 13n, 14n, 16, 19-21, 22n, 26n, 28-29, 32, 42n, 44, 48, 50-53, 52n, 58; Bruce Wayne 13, 19-20, 57
*Batman* (comic books and movies) 12-13, 21n, 29n
Bible 2, 4, 6-7, 7n, 15, 36, 38-40, 42, 49n, 50, 56, 65, 91, 97, 100
bi-gendered 38-39
Black Widow (character) 45, 94, 96-97, 99-100

Campbell, Joseph 10, 23n
Captain America (character) 11, 19, 21-22, 24, 24n, 29-32, 50-51, 51n, 101
*Captain America* (comic books and movies) 30, 30n, 50
Chesterton, G. K. 3, 7, 17
Christ 7, 9n, 10-11, 14, 16n, 18-24, 19n, 29, 33, 37, 47, 47n, 59n, 63-66, 68, 70-74; Messiah 11, 20, 69, 70n; Redeemer 29, 73
Christianity 1, 9n, 36-37, 43n, 48, 60, 97, 107-109
Christ-type 7, 16, 19-20, 19n, 21n, 22, 22n, 26, 28, 61, 66, 68-69, 70n, 72-74, 100n
Cicero 3n
comic books 2, 11-12, 11n, 15, 17, 44, 57-58, 67, 74, 77, 84, 85n, 103, 104n, 107, 109n, 113, 122
Comics Code 17, 30, 46n, 51, 51n, 58
Cooper, John 37
cosmic beings (characters) 89, 91-93, 92n, 95-97, 104n

creation 4-6, 8, 10, 35, 47n, 53, 56, 63-64, 72, 90-91, 91n, 93, 98, 120-121
cross-dressing 49n
cultural mandate 4

Daredevil (character) 13n, 14, 14n, 19, 51, 54, 100
the DC universe 13, 25, 28-29, 32, 39, 42, 65n, 81
DiPaolo, Marc 18n, 30n, 46n
disability 35, 43, 53-56, 53n, 59-60
DNA 54, 54n, 56, 105-106, 108-109
Doctor Strange (character) 11, 89-90, 98, 115-116
dragon 10, 13, 109
duty 18, 26, 32, 35, 44, 46-47, 52, 52n, 55, 60, 67, 85, 87, 101, 111, 114n, 117-118

Earth 4-5, 14, 20, 20n, 22-23, 26, 28, 50, 53, 58, 65-66, 70-71, 73-74, 83-86, 89n, 92, 94, 96-97, 98n, 105, 122
Eco, Umberto 66
elders (characters) 92-97, 92n, 100, 104n
emotion 4, 9, 54, 57, 59, 62, 77, 80, 82-83, 86, 98, 109, 120, 122
essence 38-42, 44, 47n, 48, 54n, 90, 97, 101, 103-108, 111

essentialism 38, 44n
evidence 1-3, 12, 18, 20, 39-41, 43, 56, 84, 108, 117
evolution 15, 15n, 66, 107n

the Fall (human) 10, 18, 20, 29, 33, 43, 53-54, 54n, 56, 59, 119-120
the Fantastic Four (characters) 13n, 14, 29, 31, 50n, 89, 99
femininity (feminine) 7, 37-49, 40n, 42n, 47n, 48n, 51n, 52-53, 53n, 58, 58n, 60; womanly 48, 60
feminism 36, 38, 44-46, 46n, 49
fornication 49-51, 51n; sex before marriage 50-51, 60
Frazer, James 3, 3n
free will 40, 87, 91, 91n, 99, 102, 108-109, 115, 119-120, 122
Freud, Sigmund 3

gender 35-50, 43n, 44n, 48n, 49n, 52-55, 54n, 58-60
gene 55-57, 96, 104-106, 110-111
general revelation 2, 56
giant 12, 44, 79, 92-93
God 2n, 4-8, 9n, 10n, 11, 13-15, 13n, 14n, 15n, 20, 22, 26, 33, 35-41, 38n, 39n, 41n, 43-44, 44n, 47-48, 47n, 50-53, 54n, 55-57, 55n,

60-62, 64-66, 69, 71-73, 79, 86, 89-91, 91n, 93, 95-103, 98n, 102n, 104n, 105-106, 111-112, 114-122; as the Creator 4-5, 14, 35, 90-91, 97, 102, 114-115; as the Good 6, 62, 68n, 90, 98-102, 119-120; as Love 36, 114-115

gods 2n, 3n, 6-7, 9n, 10-16, 11n, 20n, 23, 28, 33n, 37, 39-41, 44-45, 72-73, 73n, 89-90, 92-102, 93n, 98n, 104n

Green Arrow (character) 27n, 50, 60, 60n

Green Lantern (character) 13n, 14, 28-29, 53, 58, 58n, 77-78, 81-87; Alan Scott 16, 58, 58n, 82, 82n, 86; Hal Jordan 81-86

*Green Lantern* (comic books and movies) 15, 50, 81

Grayling, A. C. 70

Guardians (*Green Lantern*) 15, 28, 77-78, 81-87

happiness 27n, 48, 62, 69, 79-81, 85, 87, 115, 117-118

happy ending 10

Heaven 6, 10, 13-15, 24n, 32, 36, 41, 66, 69, 73, 73n, 89, 89n, 91n, 98, 101, 109, 121

Hell 13, 15-16, 16n, 27n, 98n, 121

Hercules 7, 13-14, 22, 92-95

hermaphrodite 54n

hero 10-13, 11n, 16-20, 21n, 22-24, 22n, 23n, 30n, 33, 35, 44, 46n, 50-52, 58, 64, 64n, 66, 70, 73n, 74, 84, 100-101, 103-106, 104n, 111, 115, 117; heroics 14, 15n, 46, 50, 52-53, 60, 66, 86, 90, 110n, 111, 114n

homosexual act 57-58, 59n, 60;

homosexual orientation 35, 53-60, 59n, 60n

the Hulk (character) 11, 14, 29, 48, 48n, 50, 94-100, 103-104, 104n, 106n, 107n, 109n, 110n, 111n; Bruce Banner 94, 100, 103, 104, 106n, 107, 111n

*Hulk* (comic books and movies) 11, 15, 48n, 103-104, 104n, 107, 107n, 109, 109n, 110n, 111-112

identity 20n, 25, 43, 55, 66, 72; personal identity 103-104, 104n, 106; secret identity 20

immodesty 49, 60

injustice 4, 20, 22, 28, 32, 51, 57, 59-60, 78, 102n, 115-116, 119, 121-122; evil 4, 6-7, 10-11, 13, 16, 18-19, 21, 21n, 30, 30n, 45, 59, 61, 67, 72, 77, 81-87, 98-100, 114-116,

118-122, 119n; sin 4, 20, 22, 42, 56-57, 87, 100, 102n, 116, 119-121
Iron Man (character) 20, 29, 31, 51n, 101

Jesus 9-10, 19, 21, 25-26, 29, 36, 40-41, 44, 55-56, 63-67, 64n, 65n, 67n, 69-74, 90-91, 97, 99, 100n, 113-114, 116, 121-122; also see Christ
Jew 30, 35, 64, 104, 108-109; Jewish 22, 25, 29, 63, 104
the Joker 21n, 29, 50
justice 18, 20-23, 20n, 21n, 25-28, 46, 50, 58, 66-67, 69-71, 78-79, 87, 100, 113, 115-122
the Justice League (characters) 14, 25, 28
*The Justice League* (comic books and movies) 11, 11n, 53, 67

*kalam* cosmological argument 14
Kant, Immanuel 62
king 6, 10, 15, 20, 28, 36-37, 65n, 79-81, 91-93, 92n, 93n
Knowles, Christopher 11, 11n, 23, 23n, 73n

Lawrence, John (Shelton) 18, 19n, 27n, 30n, 73n
Lee, Ang 103-110, 107n, 109n, 112

Lee, Stan 11n, 23n, 50, 90, 104, 104n
LeVay, Simon 55
Lewis, C. S. 2n, 3, 3n, 5n, 6-9, 6n, 8n, 10n, 15, 15n, 37-38
the Living Tribunal (character) 89, 91, 95-96, 104n
Loki 38-39, 44n, 60, 95, 100n
Luthor, Lex 13, 28, 63-64, 68, 73

MacIntyre, Alasdair 27n
Macrobius 3, 3n
Madrid, Mike 44, 46n, 48, 51
magic 32, 42n, 45, 79, 94-95, 115
marriage 37, 47n, 49-52, 51n, 55, 58-60, 59n, 118; gay marriage 58-60
Marston, William Moulton 45-46
Martian Manhunter (character) 15, 39, 44n, 59n
the Marvel universe 13-15, 13n, 25, 29-32, 35, 38-39, 41-42, 44n, 60, 89-90, 92-93, 92n, 95-99, 98n, 102, 102n, 104n, 116
masculinity 38-40, 47, 47n, 50-51, 60; masculine 35-42, 40n, 42n, 44-53, 47n, 48n, 53n, 58, 58n, 60; manly 47-52, 58, 60
mercy 18, 22, 62, 64, 100-

101, 121-122
metaphysical naturalism  8, 15, 103-106, 109, 111-112
Miller, Frank  12, 12n, 41n
Moreland, J. P.  6n, 40n, 41n
Morrison, Grant  11n, 14, 33n, 64n
Ms. Marvel (character)  12
mystery  69, 89n
mythology  1-3, 2n, 3n, 6-7, 9-11, 10n, 11n, 14-16, 15n, 23-24, 35-36, 39, 44-45, 48, 60, 66, 68n, 70, 73n, 90, 92-93, 93n; myth  2-3, 2n, 3n, 5-12, 6n, 9n, 14, 15n, 16-18, 19n, 20, 23, 23n, 35, 51, 54, 64, 66, 69-70, 79
Müller, Max  3, 3n

the Natural Law  7, 20, 21n, 56, 57n, 103, 106, 111-112; as *Asha* 6; as Ma'at 7; as *Rita* 6; as *Tao* 6; as the universal moral law 61-62, 64, 67-68, 117
Nietzsche, Friedrich  25, 61-64, 66, 68-69, 73-74, 77, 80, 87; will-to-power  77, 80, 87

Odin  6, 93-94, 96, 98
omnipotence  2n, 36, 39, 118
orphan  19

*Paradise Lost*  9

patriotism  26-27, 27n
St. Paul  24, 28, 40, 60n
perfection  10, 32, 74, 79-80, 114-115, 122
philosophy  1-2, 2n, 23, 57n, 62, 93, 104n, 113
Piper, John  41n, 47-48, 47n
Plantinga, Alvin  120n
Plato  2, 2n, 5, 8, 29, 56n, 61, 68n, 73, 78-85, 87, 93
politics  18n, 26, 28-29, 31, 59n, 84
power  7-8, 12, 13n, 17, 23n, 26-28, 30, 32, 36, 44-46, 53, 61-64, 66, 68, 70, 72-73, 77-87, 89-91, 93-99, 98n, 103, 105, 110, 113-114, 114n, 116-119, 122-123
prayer  14, 37, 115, 117
the problem of evil  118-119, 122
Professor X (character)  23, 42, 54
propaganda  18n, 30n, 45

redemption  10, 53
responsibility  47, 77, 113, 114n, 116-117, 119, 122-123
Reynolds, Richard  11
Robin (character)  13, 52-53, 53n, 58n
the Romantics  8

saint  24, 24n
Satan  6-7, 10, 40, 44n, 65n, 68, 97-98; Devil 13, 15-16, 15n, 40n, 98, 110

Sax, Leonard  43, 43n, 47
the School of Chartres  3, 3n
sex  37-38, 41-43, 44n, 46, 54n, 55, 60; act of  44, 50-52, 51n, 60
sexual orientation  35, 53, 55-57
Shuster, Joe  25, 61, 63-64, 74
Siegel, Jerry  25, 61, 63-64, 74
sky fathers (characters)  93-97, 104n
soul  3n, 5, 38-43, 42n, 43n, 44n, 47-49, 53-56, 54n, 58, 60, 68, 80-81, 83-84, 96n, 97, 99, 104-112, 116; spirit  13, 38-42, 44, 51-52, 97, 99, 104, 106-109, 118
Spider-Man (character)  12, 13n, 14, 20, 29, 31, 33, 44, 51, 89-90, 89n, 113, 122-123, 122n; Peter Parker  12, 19-20, 36, 48n, 90, 113-115, 118
*Spider-Man* (comic books and movies)  12, 30, 33, 48, 99, 113, 115-119, 121-123, 122n
sub-creator  4-5, 96
substance  38-39, 44n, 104, 104n, 107, 111
Supergirl (character)  13n, 14, 44, 48, 69
super-human  5-9, 11-13, 15, 19, 23, 24n, 94-97, 105, 116
Superman (character)  14, 20-21, 20n, 21n, 22n, 24n, 25-33, 26n, 27n, 44, 46n, 48, 51-53, 53n, 61, 63-74, 65n, 68n, 73n, 74n, 86; Clark Kent  19-20, 51n, 65, 72
*Superman* (comic books and movies)  13n, 14-15, 17-18, 21n, 22n, 26 26n, 27n, 46n, 64n, 65, 65n, 68-74, 68n, 70n, 73n
super-natural (supernatural)  3, 5, 7, 11
symbol  16, 25-26, 28-29, 31-32, 61, 68, 70-71, 74, 101

Thor (character)  7, 11, 11n, 13, 29, 31, 50-51, 89, 89n, 91n, 92, 94-96, 98n, 99-101
*Thor* (comic books and movies)  89n, 91n, 100n
Tolkien, J. R. R.  3-7, 9n, 10, 14, 16
truth  1-2, 2n, 7-9, 22, 26-28, 30, 32, 36, 38, 47, 62, 66-67, 69-70, 105, 107, 110

vigilante  11n, 25n, 33n
villain  11, 13, 18, 21-22, 21n, 25, 30n, 31, 50-51, 50n, 51n, 54n, 64, 65n, 68, 72, 74, 84, 99-100, 103, 105-106, 110
violence  17, 49-50; against women  49
virtue  16, 27, 27n, 32, 45,

48, 56, 81

the Wasp  45, 50, 94-97,
    99-101
*Watchmen*  21, 21n, 81
Wertham, Fredric  17, 48,
    58, 63, 74
willpower  77, 79, 82-83,
    85, 87
wisdom  7, 19, 21, 28, 52,
    65n, 80-85, 117
Wolverine (character)  15-
    16, 16n, 54
Wonder Woman (character)
    13n, 14, 22, 22n, 28-
    30, 32, 44n, 45-49,
    46n, 53, 58, 67
*Wonder Woman* (comic
    books and movies)
    22n, 44n, 46

*X-men* (comic books and
    movies)  14, 16, 21n,
    29, 42, 50, 54-56, 54n,
    59n

Zeus  2n, 6, 14, 20n, 92-93,
    95, 100

# Other Books of Interest

## C. S. Lewis

*C. S. Lewis: Views From Wake Forest - Essays on C. S. Lewis*
Michael Travers, editor

Contains sixteen scholarly presentations from the international C. S. Lewis convention in Wake Forest, NC. Walter Hooper shares his important essay "Editing C. S. Lewis," a chronicle of publishing decisions after Lewis' death in 1963.

*"Scholars from a variety of disciplines address a wide range of issues. The happy result is a fresh and expansive view of an author who well deserves this kind of thoughtful attention."*
      Diana Pavlac Glyer, author of *The Company They Keep*

*The Hidden Story of Narnia:*
*A Book-By-Book Guide to Lewis' Spiritual Themes*
Will Vaus

A book of insightful commentary equally suited for teens or adults – Will Vaus points out connections between the *Narnia* books and spiritual/biblical themes, as well as between ideas in the *Narnia* books and C. S. Lewis' other books. Learn what Lewis himself said about the overarching and unifying thematic structure of the Narnia books. That is what this book explores; what C. S. Lewis called "the hidden story" of Narnia. Each chapter includes questions for individual use or small group discussion.

*Why I Believe in Narnia:*
*33 Reviews and Essays on the Life and Work of C.S. Lewis*
James Como

Chapters range from reviews of critical books, documentaries and movies to evaluations of Lewis' books to biographical analysis.

*"A valuable, wide-ranging collection of essays by one of the best informed and most accute commentators on Lewis' work and ideas."*
      Peter Schakel, author of *Imagination & the Arts in C.S. Lewis*

*C. S. Lewis Goes to Heaven: A Reader's Guide to The Great Divorce*
David G. Clark

This is the first book devoted solely to this often neglected book and the first to reveal several important secrets Lewis concealed within the story. Lewis felt his imaginary trip to Hell and Heaven was far better than his book *The Screwtape Letters*, which has become a classic. Clark is an ordained minister who has taught courses on Lewis for more than 30 years and is a New Testament and Greek scholar with a Doctor of Philosophy degree in Biblical Studies from the University of Notre Dame. Readers will discover the many literary and biblical influences Lewis utilized in writing his brilliant novel.

MORE INFORMATION AT WWW.WINGEDLIONPRESS.COM

*C. S. Lewis & Philosophy as a Way of Life*
Adam Barkman

C. S. Lewis is rarely thought of as a "philosopher" per se despite having both studied and taught philosophy for several years at Oxford. Lewis's long journey to Christianity was essentially philosophical – passing through seven different stages. This 624 page book is an invaluable reference for C. S. Lewis scholars and fans alike

*C. S. Lewis: His Literary Achievement*
Colin Manlove

*"This is a positively brilliant book, written with splendor, elegance, profundity and evidencing an enormous amount of learning. This is probably not a book to give a first-time reader of Lewis. But for those who are more broadly read in the Lewis corpus this book is an absolute gold mine of information. The author gives us a magnificent overview of Lewis' many writings, tracing for us thoughts and ideas which recur throughout, and at the same time telling us how each book differs from the others. I think it is not extravagant to call C. S. Lewis: His Literary Achievement a tour de force."*
　　　　　　　　Robert Merchant, *St. Austin Review*, Book Review Editor

*Mythopoeic Narnia: Memory, Metaphor, and Metamorphoses in C. S. Lewis's The Chronicles of Narnia*
Salwa Khoddam

Dr. Khoddam, the founder of the C. S. Lewis and Inklings Society (2004), has been teaching university courses using Lewis' books for over 25 years. Her book offers a fresh approach to the *Narnia* books based on an inquiry into Lewis' readings and use of classical and Christian symbols. She explores the literary and intellectual contexts of these stories, the traditional myths and motifs, and places them in the company of the greatest Christian mythopoeic works of Western literature. In Lewis' imagination, memory and metaphor interact to advance his purpose – a Christian metamorphosis. *Mythopoeic Narnia* helps to open the door for readers into the magical world of the Western imagination.

*Speaking of Jack: A C. S. Lewis Discussion Guide*
Will Vaus

C. S. Lewis societies have been forming around the world since the first one started in New York City in 1969. Will Vaus has started and led three groups himself. *Speaking of Jack* is the result of Vaus' experience in leading those Lewis societies. Included here are introductions to most of Lewis' books as well as questions designed to stimulate discussion about Lewis' life and work. These materials have been "road-tested" with real groups made up of young and old, some very familiar with Lewis and some newcomers. *Speaking of Jack* may be used in an existing book discussion group, to start a C. S. Lewis society, or to guide your own exploration of Lewis' books.

# George MacDonald

*Diary of an Old Soul & The White Page Poems*
George MacDonald and Betty Aberlin

The first edition of George MacDonald's book of daily poems included a blank page opposite each page of poems. Readers were invited to write their own reflections on the "white page." MacDonald wrote: "Let your white page be ground, my print be seed, growing to golden ears, that faith and hope may feed." Betty Aberlin responded to MacDonald's invitation with daily poems of her own.

*"Betty Aberlin's close readings of George MacDonald's verses and her thoughtful responses to them speak clearly of her poetic gifts and spiritual intelligence."*
    Luci Shaw, poet

*George MacDonald: Literary Heritage and Heirs*
Roderick McGillis, editor

This latest collection of 14 essays sets a new standard that will influence MacDonald studies for many more years. George MacDonald experts are increasingly evaluating his entire corpus within the nineteenth century context.

*"This comprehensive collection represents the best of contemporary scholarship on George MacDonald."*
    Rolland Hein, author of *George MacDonald: Victorian Mythmaker*

*In the Near Loss of Everything: George MacDonald's Son in America*
Dale Wayne Slusser

In the summer of 1887, George MacDonald's son Ronald, newly engaged to artist Louise Blandy, sailed from England to America to teach school. The next summer he returned to England to marry Louise and bring her back to America. On August 27, 1890, Louise died, leaving him with an infant daughter. Ronald once described losing a beloved spouse as "the near loss of everything." Dale Wayne Slusser unfolds this poignant story with unpublished letters and photos that give readers a glimpse into the close-knit MacDonald family. Also included is Ronald's essay about his father, *George MacDonald: A Personal Note*, plus a selection from Ronald's 1922 fable, *The Laughing Elf*, about the necessity of both sorrow and joy in life.

*A Novel Pulpit: Sermons From George MacDonald's Fiction*
David L. Neuhouser

"In MacDonald's novels, the Christian teaching emerges out of the characters and story line, the narrator's comments, and inclusion of sermons given by the fictional preachers. The sermons in the novels are shorter than the ones in collections of MacDonald's sermons and so are perhaps more accessible for some. In any case, they are both stimulating and thought-provoking. This collection of sermons from ten novels serve to bring out the 'freshness and brilliance' of MacDonald's message."
    From the author's introduction

# Pop Culture

*To Love Another Person: A Spiritual Journey Through Les Miserables*
John Morrison

The powerful story of Jean Valjean's redemption is beloved by readers and theater goers everywhere. In this companion and guide to Victor Hugo's masterpiece, author John Morrison unfolds the spiritual depth and breadth of this classic novel and broadway musical.

*Through Common Things: Philosophical Reflections on Popular Culture*
Adam Barkman

"Barkman presents us with an amazingly wide-ranging collection of philosophical reflections grounded in the everyday things of popular culture – past and present, eastern and western, factual and fictional. Throughout his encounters with often surprising subject-matter (the value of darkness?), he writes clearly and concisely, moving seamlessly between Aristotle and anime, Lord Buddha and Lord Voldemort.... This is an informative and entertaining book to read!"
          Doug Bloomberg, Professor of Philosophy, Institute for Christian Studies

*Spotlight:*
*A Close-up Look at the Artistry and Meaning of Stephenie Meyer's Twilight Novels*
John Granger

Stephenie Meyer's *Twilight* saga has taken the world by storm. But is there more to *Twilight* than a love story for teen girls crossed with a cheesy vampire-werewolf drama? *Spotlight* reveals the literary backdrop, themes, artistry, and meaning of the four Bella Swan adventures. *Spotlight* is the perfect gift for serious *Twilight* readers.

*Virtuous Worlds: The Video Gamer's Guide to Spiritual Truth*
John Stanifer

Popular titles like *Halo 3* and *The Legend of Zelda: Twilight Princess* fly off shelves at a mind-blowing rate. John Stanifer, an avid gamer, shows readers specific parallels between Christian faith and the content of their favorite games. Written with wry humor (including a heckler who frequently pokes fun at the author) this book will appeal to gamers and non-gamers alike. Those unfamiliar with video games may be pleasantly surprised to find that many elements in those "virtual worlds" also qualify them as "virtuous worlds."

# Memoir

*Called to Serve: Life as a Firefighter-Deacon*
Deacon Anthony R. Surozenski

*Called to Serve* is the story of one man's dream to be a firefighter. But dreams have a way of taking detours – so Tony Soruzenski became a teacher and eventually a volunteer firefighter. And when God enters the picture, Tony is faced with a choice. Will he give up firefighting to follow another call? After many years, Tony's two callings are finally united – in service as a fire chaplain at Ground Zero after the 9-11 attacks and in other ways he could not have imagined. Tony is Chief Chaplain's aid for the Massachusetts Corp of Fire Chaplains and Director for the Office of the Diaconate of the Diocese of Worchester, Massachusettes.

# Harry Potter

*The Order of Harry Potter: The Literary Skill of the Hogwarts Epic*
Colin Manlove

Colin Manlove, a popular conference speaker and author of over a dozen books, has earned an international reputation as an expert on fantasy and children's literature. His book, *From Alice to Harry Potter*, is a survey of 400 English fantasy books. In *The Order of Harry Potter*, he compares and contrasts *Harry Potter* with works by "Inklings" writers J.R.R. Tolkien, C.S. Lewis and Charles Williams; he also examines Rowling's treatment of the topic of imagination; her skill in organization and the use of language; and the book's underlying motifs and themes.

*Harry Potter & Imagination: The Way Between Two Worlds*
Travis Prinzi

Imaginative literature places a reader between two worlds: the story world and the world of daily life, and challenges the reader to imagine and to act for a better world. Starting with discussion of Harry Potter's more important themes, *Harry Potter & Imagination* takes readers on a journey through the transformative power of those themes for both the individual and for culture by placing Rowling's series in its literary, historical, and cultural contexts.

*Repotting Harry Potter: A Professor's Guide for the Serious Re-Reader*
*Rowling Revisited: Return Trips to Harry, Fantastic Beasts, Quidditch, & Beedle the Bard*
James W. Thomas

In *Repotting Harry Potter* and his sequel book *Rowling Revisited*, Dr. James W. Thomas points out the humor, puns, foreshadowing and literary parallels in the Potter books. In *Rowling Revisted*, readers will especially find useful three extensive appendixes – "Fantastic Beasts and the Pages Where You'll Find Them," "Quidditch Through the Pages," and "The Books in the Potter Books." Dr. Thomas makes re-reading the Potter books even more rewarding and enjoyable.

*Deathly Hallows Lectures:*
*The Hogwarts Professor Explains Harry's Final Adventure*
John Granger

In *The Deathly Hallows Lectures*, John Granger reveals the finale's brilliant details, themes, and meanings. *Harry Potter* fans will be surprised by and delighted with Granger's explanations of the three dimensions of meaning in *Deathly Hallows*. Ms. Rowling has said that alchemy sets the "parameters of magic" in the series; after reading the chapter-length explanation of *Deathly Hallows* as the final stage of the alchemical Great Work, the serious reader will understand how important literary alchemy is in understanding Rowling's artistry and accomplishment.

*Hog's Head Conversations: Essays on Harry Potter*
Travis Prinzi, Editor

Ten fascinating essays on Harry Potter by popular Potter writers and speakers including John Granger, James W. Thomas, Colin Manlove, and Travis Prinzi.

# Poets and Poetry

*Remembering Roy Campbell: The Memoirs of his Daughters, Anna and Tess*
Introduction by Judith Lütge Coullie, Editor
Preface by Joseph Pearce

Anna and Teresa Campbell were the daughters of the handsome young South African poet and writer, Roy Campbell (1901-1957), and his beautiful English wife, Mary Garman. In their frank and moving memoirs, Anna and Tess recall the extraordinary, and often very difficult, lives they shared with their exceptional parents. The book includes over 50 photos, 344 footnotes, a timeline of Campbell's life, and a complete index.

*In the Eye of the Beholder: How to See the World Like a Romantic Poet*
Louis Markos

Born out of the French Revolution and its radical faith that a nation could be shaped and altered by the dreams and visions of its people, British Romantic Poetry was founded on a belief that the objects and realities of our world, whether natural or human, are not fixed in stone but can be molded and transformed by the visionary eye of the poet. Unlike many of the books written on Romanticism, which devote many pages to the poets and few pages to their poetry, the focus here is firmly on the poems themselves. The author thereby draws the reader intimately into the life of these poems. A separate bibliographical essay is provided for readers listing accessible biographies of each poet and critical studies of their work.

*The Cat on the Catamaran: A Christmas Tale*
John Martin

Here is a modern-day parable of a modern-day cat with modern-day attitudes. Riverboat Dan is a "cool" cat on a perpetual vacation from responsibility. He's *The Cat on the Catamaran* – sailing down the river of life. Dan keeps his guilty conscience from interfering with his fun until he runs into trouble. But will he have the courage to believe that it's never too late to change course? (For ages 10 to adult)

*"Cat lovers and poetry lovers alike will enjoy this whimsical story about Riverboat Dan, a philosophical cat in search of meaning."*
        Regina Doman, author of *Angel in the Water*

# Fiction

*The Iona Conspiracy (from The Remnant Chronicles book series)*
Gary Gregg

Readers find themselves on a modern adventure through ancient Celtic myth and legend as thirteen year old Jacob uncovers his destiny within "the remnant" of the Sporrai Order. As the Iona Academy comes under the control of educational reformers and ideological scientists, Jacob finds himself on a dangerous mission to the sacred Scottish island of Iona and discovers how his life is wrapped up with the fate of the long lost cover of *The Book of Kells*. From its connections to Arthurian legend to references to real-life people, places, and historical mysteries, *Iona* is an adventure that speaks to eternal truths as well as the challenges of the modern world. A young adult novel, *Iona* can be enjoyed by the entire family.

www.ingramcontent.com/pod-product-compliance
Lightning Source LLC
Chambersburg PA
CBHW031155020426
42333CB00013B/681